BACKSTAGE

Also by Donna Leon

The Jewels of Paradise
My Venice and Other Essays
Wandering Through Life: A Memoir

Commissario Brunetti Mysteries

Death at La Fenice

Death in a Strange Country

The Anonymous Venetian

A Venetian Reckoning

Acqua Alta

The Death of Faith

A Noble Radiance

Fatal Remedies

Friends in High Places

A Sea of Troubles

Wilful Behaviour

Uniform Justice

Doctored Evidence

Blood from a Stone

Through a Glass, Darkly

Suffer the Little Children

The Girl of His Dreams

About Face

A Question of Belief

Drawing Conclusions

Beastly Things

The Golden Egg

By Its Cover

Falling in Love

The Waters of Eternal Youth

Earthly Remains

The Temptation of Forgiveness

Unto Us a Son Is Given

Trace Elements

Transient Desires

Give Unto Others

So Shall You Reap

A Refiner's Fire

BACKSTAGE

STORIES OF A WRITING LIFE

DONNA
LEON

Atlantic Monthly Press
New York

First published in Great Britain in 2025 by Hutchinson Heinemann, an imprinit of Penguin Random House

Printed in the United States of America

Typeset in 10.4/15pt Palatino LT Pro by Jouve (UK), Milton Keynes

First Grove Atlantic hardcover edition: August 2025

Library of Congress Cataloging-in-Publication data is available for this title.

ISBN 978-0-8021-6537-4
eISBN 978-0-8021-6538-1

Atlantic Monthly Press
an imprint of Grove Atlantic
154 West 14th Street
New York, NY 10011

Distributed by Publishers Group West

groveatlantic.com

25 26 27 28   10 9 8 7 6 5 4 3 2 1

For Anna and Frank Bonitatibus

This is life: people are strange. And from that comes the realization that, to many people reading our character, we can seem just as strange.

Contents

Early in Life

Cedric   3
Tell 'Em Anything   12
Jack and Jill   21

Heroes

Getting Zapped   29
Detectives and Villains   35
Orlando's a Nutcase   38

String-Pulling in Venice

The Diamond Man   45
Venice 1729   54
With a View of San Marco   61
Redentore   65

Mortal Danger

Getting Out   75
Great Expectations   85
Regina   88

CONTENTS

Trips

San Gennaro   101
Master and Commander   109
The Beauty of the Unknown   116

Behind the Scene

A New Case for Brunetti   123
On the Move   127
With a Little Help from Lew Archer   132

Amorality

Dirt   137
Janus-Faced Deity   144
A Complex Character   155

Love

Dear Guido   161
Gardening   163
A Book of a Lifetime   167

Moment of Truth

The Death of Ivan Ilych   171
The Big Bow Wow   175
Show, Don't Tell   180

CONTENTS

Ends

The Big Sleep   191
Loneliness   196
Addio   201
In Memoriam   205

Early in Life

Cedric

Although he might be well into his sixties by now, my guess is that Cedric, according to statistics, is probably either dead or imprisoned. Cedric was Black and lived in America, so the odds were against him from the beginning. From long before the beginning, it might be clearer to say.

I met him in the 1970s, when I was in my thirties, living in Bloomfield, New Jersey, and attending night classes to finish my master's degree in English Literature. I supported myself by working as a substitute teacher in the elementary schools of Newark, New Jersey, a city that had the highest infant mortality rate in the country. It was about ten kilometres from where I lived, but it might as well have been on the moon, so different was Newark from the cities around it.

Cedric was one of the students in a third-grade class I was asked to teach for a month. He must have been ten, no more than that, and thin, as if his body had decided to use the energy available to it to grow tall, even if he had to be thin to do so. His skin was medium brown, and he had curly dark hair, cut very short. His eyes were a bit lighter than his hair, and his hands were never still. His smile, which I suspect appeared only by accident, was lovely yet somehow guarded: his normal expression was a worried nervousness, something that belonged anywhere but on the face of a ten-year-old.

The school in which I taught was made of red brick, just like the school in the third-grade 'reader' we used. It was in a city that even then had a majority Black population, although the city government was still in the hands of the descendants of the millions of Italians who emigrated to the US in the early twentieth century.

The Black population, far greater in number than the white, had no political clout. This was the US in the 70s, and that was the way things were, even though the Black residents had rioted for days only three years before. His Honour the Mayor had recently been convicted of conspiracy and extortion and was currently serving time as a guest of the state, but Newark being the kind of place it was, such things did not disturb the citizens of the city, and surely not the members of the faculty of the Franklin School.

There were about thirty kids in the class I was given to teach, not that I had any idea of what third-graders were expected to know, nor was any suggestion provided that might have advised me how to teach them. Half of the kids were girls, half boys; most of them were Black.

Some background information is needed here. There had been one Black student in my own elementary school

class, none in my high school or university classes. I had
no Black friends because segregation worked and kept
us far apart, as separated and incomprehensible as creatures of different species. Protest against racial injustice
was seen, by white people, entirely on television, it being
a reality they did not suffer. The few times I'd travelled in
the South, visiting family, I'd been startled by signs indi-
cating that certain drinking fountains, buses, restaurants,
beaches and just about any place where humans congre-
gated were strictly segregated. The only explanation I
could wrest from my parents, people of a liberal cast of
mind, was a falsely neutral, 'People are different down
here.' I might as well have been living in Cape Town.

I was the grandchild of immigrants. My family name
was once de León, but both the 'de' and the accent disappeared at the port where my paternal grandfather
entered the United States from a South American country
the name of which he never mentioned. Nor did he ever
speak to any of his grandchildren in Spanish. He came,
he saw, he started down the gangplank, and by the time
he got to the bottom and stepped away from the boat, he
was American and accepted as such. Because he was a
well-educated and successful businessman, and because
he looked like everyone else, he was never the victim of
prejudice of any sort, nor did his grandchildren, sheared
free of that foreign name, even know what prejudice was.

Cedric, born American, had none of these advan-
tages. Often absent from class (we didn't have to report a

student's absence until the third day), when he did come, he usually sat and looked out the window. As I recall, he was always eager to be the one to read out loud from the prescribed 'reader', within whose pages Jack and Jill went up the hill and Farmer Brown loved his cows. He read aloud in a clear voice, had no difficulty in pronouncing words, and added a note of drama to the voices of the various characters. These were his good days.

I came to recognize and profit from them by asking the class if they wanted Cedric to be the first reader that day. Other days he came and sat at his desk, looking out the window and not participating in any of the activities except the single hour of outside exercise, when the boys gave an example of what appeared to be demonic possession and the girls sat on a long bench and talked to one another. And then there were the bad days, perhaps one a week, when he would – with no apparent reason – fall into a frenzy of violence, always careful to choose to start a fight with a student larger and stronger than himself.

At the beginning of my second week, Cedric began to materialize in the lot where I parked my car and walked with me to the school. Twice he took my hand and held it until we were one street from the school, when he disappeared.

It took me only a few days to realize that the kids and I lived, and had always lived, on different planets. I was a middle-class white woman upon whom life had showered uncountable blessings, while these were poor kids who wore the same clothes to school all week and devoured the school lunch in minutes. Just as fish don't take samples of the water in which they swim, most people then didn't – and I fear don't now – pay attention to the rules underpinning the society in which they lived.

I'd grown up no more than ten kilometres from where Cedric lived. While I was learning how to distinguish a Shakespearean sonnet from a Spenserian one, he was mapping out the violent territory in which he lived.

One morning during my last week with this class, one of the other boys told me that Cedric, who had apparently raised the calibre of his anger, had brought a knife to school, saying he was going to stab another student. When I asked Cedric to give me the knife – I wasted no time with questions – he slapped first his right hand, then his left on his pocket while heatedly maintaining his innocence.

I held out my palm, and after very little resistance, he handed me a pocket knife with a blade long enough to peel a grape. He then surprised me, and the other students, by walking across the room and standing behind the open door of the classroom, as if he had acknowledged his guilt and would now begin serving his sentence.

Two boys at the front of the room used this distraction to start screaming at one another, and then they were rolling around on the floor without appearing to want to do much damage to each other. I pulled them to their feet just as the three o'clock dismissal bell rang, and never had even the voices of angels been so sweet and welcome.

The kids lined up, careful to let the girls go first, and filed quietly out of the room and down the stairs, leaving me behind. They did not erupt until they were outside the building, but by then it was after three and they were no longer my responsibility. Incapable of motion, I stood and stared at the closet doors at the back of the room, where posters of Lenni-Lenape Indians showed the original owners of the land now called New Jersey. Yes, feathers in their hair, faces and bodies painted the same colour as Cedric.

Cedric.

Behind the door.

I called his name, started towards his hiding place, then stopped and said, 'Hey, Cedric, that was really a big one, huh?'

There was a shifting noise.

'You want a ride home?'

When there was no shifting noise, I added, 'I'm beat. You must be tired, too.'

There might have been a noise, so I asked, 'You wanna help me close the windows?'

The door moved as he slipped out and made towards the windows; he closed half of them carefully and silently, leaving me to take care of the higher ones. We left the school together, both of us wearing jackets and scarves against the autumn chill. He must have known where the car was, for he led the way, and once we both got into the red VW, I asked him to tell me how to get to his home.

'Left. Now right. Up there on the right there's a place to park.' There was, and I did.

We got out. He closed the door carefully, no slamming. I did the same.

The houses were all the same: narrow, wooden, paint peeling everywhere, steps cracked, more peeling paint.

He pulled out a key on a chain he wore under his jacket and turned it in the lock. He opened the door and stepped back to let me enter first. More peeling paint and one or two wobbly steps, a very untrustworthy railing.

My brother once kept hamsters. The smell was the same: powerful, chemical, rich with urea. Cedric stopped on the second floor and knocked a few soft times at the door on the left.

A noise came through the door, a key turned, then another higher up, and then it was pulled open. She was stunned by the sight of me and failed to hide it. Her expression opened with fear, moved to suspicion, and finally settled into curiosity. She was tall; her eyes and mouth left no doubt that she was Cedric's mother.

'This is my teacher,' he said.

Her face softened, as at the removal of peril.

'Would you like to come in, ma'am? Can I get you a glass of water?'

I gave what I thought was a smile and said, 'Thank you, ma'am, but I've got to go back to the school. Forgot some papers.'

As if I'd not spoken, his mother pulled the door fully

open and stepped back. The room was spotless, cleaner than my own living room, and far neater, but the smell had followed us upstairs and inside.

There was a call from the other room. She looked at Cedric, made a calculation, and said, 'You go take a look at the twins, Cedric.'

'Yes, Mom,' he said and walked towards the voice that was calling again.

When he had stepped into the other room, his mother looked at me and asked: 'Fighting?'

I nodded.

'But he's a good boy,' she said, meaning it and making it believable. 'Sometimes some sort of devil power takes over, and he can't stop himself.'

'You talk to anyone at the school?' I asked. 'There's a nurse, isn't there?'

Her lovely face stopped being so, but all she said was, 'Yes, there's a nurse.'

Cedric came back from the other room and said the twins were OK.

'All right, then,' I said. 'Let me go get those papers.' I turned back towards the door.

'Cedric,' she said in a different, stronger voice, 'what do you do when a guest is fixin' to leave?'

'Open the door,' he said, doing just that.

'Thanks, Cedric,' I said.

Before his mother could say a word, Cedric said,

'Thanks for the ride, Teacher.' A long pause as, no doubt, he measured the risk of further words. 'That's a nice car.'

I smiled as if I believed the compliment had been partially meant for me, which I like to think was the case.

'See you tomorrow,' I said.

Outside, I stopped and looked up at what I figured was their window. Standing beside one another, they were there. They both waved, and I waved back.

Tell 'Em Anything

Charles Dickens is not only one of the greatest English novelists: he is a person to guide us through life with the brilliance of his wisdom. During the 70s, when I found myself without a job, it was Dickens who encouraged me to act, not mope around, hoping for a job to come looking for me. After all, 'Did anyone ever find boiled mutton and caper-sauce growing in a cocoa-nut?' No, they did not: they found it by reading job offers in *The New York Times*, where, that same day, an international company made public its search for people who taught English, asking if they would be willing to go and teach in Iran.

The alternative was a letter from the University of Massachusetts offering a fellowship that would allow me to finish my dissertation while surviving on the pennies and table scraps accompanying it, which could probably have been used to draw the whole thing out for at least three or four more years. Thus I felt the Temptation of Sloth place its heavy hand upon my shoulder and start, ever so gently, to pull me towards the warm, moist underbelly of academia.

But then, as though the heavens had parted to allow

it to reach me, the voice of Dickens intervened, stating this simple truth: 'Business first, pleasure afterwards, as King Richard the Third said when he stabbed the t'other king in the Tower, afore he smothered the babbies.' Has ever the rule of heaven been stated more clearly? 'Business first, pleasure afterwards.' I hurried home to consult the atlas, and as soon as I saw where Iran was, the deal was done, and I started my mental packing.

So far as I could tell after the first day I spent in Iran, Tehran was enormous, very noisy, and spilling over with cars, all of which were driven at excessive speed by either homicidal maniacs or the blind. The street on which the hotel was located was, for that day, even louder, for it was the holy day of Ashura, when long parades of men commemorate the death in battle of Hussein ibn Ali, the Prophet Mohammed's grandson, by chanting and beating their chests and backs. As I was later also to see in Isfahan, the very devout still flagellated themselves with chains as a sign of mourning, leaving bloody evidence of piety on the backs of their white shirts as they chanted the sad story of Hussein's death in battle.

Three months later, I'd been stationed in Isfahan and had found a place to live not far from the bazaar, a house with a mere six rooms, to keep me from feeling crowded while still sharing the space with a colleague.

The rectangular one-storey house was built of baked clay bricks and consisted of three mud-roofed rooms at each end, all faced onto a central garden with a wading pool. There were two pomegranate trees and an endless display of shiveringly ugly geraniums, all red. It was surrounded by a four-metre-high brick wall.

It was also, I was told, constructed at a certain angle, in obedience to the rules of nature. Thus, in winter, the sun, hanging low in the sky, beat down through the tall glass windows and heated the rooms at one end of the house, while by summer the arc of the sun had shifted and it shone into the rooms at the other end with such intensity that they were unbearable during the day, but the other rooms were now free of direct sunlight and rather cool.

It was possible to use a ladder to climb onto the roofs of most city houses in Isfahan and, using the flat tops of the walls as a kind of sidewalk, to walk to and fro above the various houses that shared walls. From that height it would be very easy to look down into the courtyards of your neighbours to see what they were up to. Yet in my four years in Isfahan, I never saw a person on those walkways, nor did any of my colleagues. My understanding – from both what I observed and what I was told – was always that this was not done. As simple as that. I recall little of the Farsi I learned, but one word that remains is *haram*, which means 'forbidden', strongly forbidden. Looking into your neighbour's home was *haram*.

Our landlord once had to repair the roof at the winter end of the house after it was damaged by a freak hailstorm that melted a metre-wide hole in the roof, allowing the melting mud bricks to cascade into the living room. He had the workmen there the same day, held the ladder as they climbed up to and down from the roof, always from the street outside the house, where they prepared a mixture of mud, dry grass, water, clay, sand, and what I was told was donkey dung to repair the hole. The work was done by the time the evening call to prayer sounded. He brought them back three days later, when they removed their shoes at the door to the house and painted the ceiling of the living room without ever acknowledging our presence. Had it been possible, I think they would have kept their eyes closed every minute they were in our home. The work was quickly and perfectly done.

The owner of the house, a rail-thin man seemingly in his sixties, treated us with particular respect because we were guests in his country, and we treated him with equal respect because he had earned the title '*Hajji*' for having made the pilgrimage to Mecca.

I could say little in Farsi, but he was my landlord, so my exchanges with Hajji Aragh were, however limited, cordial. He came twice a week to water the horrid geraniums, to say his prayers while facing Mecca, and then quietly to smoke a pipe of opium, after which I would offer him tea and the pistachios we kept in the house especially for him.

He held endless conversations with my roommate William, who was fluent in Farsi, and could not spend enough time with him. They would sit by the small pool – really not much bigger than a bathtub, though not as deep – and talk in soft voices, one occasionally bowing to the other, who would in turn bow back. I remember the first time they had one of these conversations, which ended when William stood, bent over, and put an envelope into the Hajji's hand. The Hajji stood in his turn and tried to push the envelope back into William's empty hands, shaking his head and speaking more loudly than he had for the last hour but doing only a mediocre job of sounding offended.

William placed his hands on his chest to show how impossible it would be to take back the envelope, and they exchanged words for a few more minutes.

Finally, the Hajji looked upwards, as if in search of advice, then conceded defeat and slipped the envelope into the front of his shirt.

William gave every sign of relief, took the Hajji's hand in his, and said '*Mamnunam*' with such sincerity that I took a step closer to see just what business he had concluded with William. The Hajji revealed nothing and bowed his way towards the door.

William accompanied the Hajji, leaving a trail of words behind him. They spent a minute at the door, and then the Hajji stepped into the lane and was gone.

Rather like the betrayed wife in a Brazilian soap opera, I waited until William was within striking distance and asked, perhaps overdoing the betrayal, anger, and jealousy, 'And what, pray tell, was *that* all about?'

Sounding far less penitent than I thought he would, William confessed, 'Paying the rent.'

The word must have passed through the neighbourhood that the *farangi* who were renting the Hajji's home did not have second heads growing under their arms, nor was there evidence in the house of the practice of any sort of demonic rite. Consequently, the quality of the almonds and pistachios we had been buying for months from the same stall in the bazaar suddenly improved; the aubergines would now last a week and no longer lie decomposed at the back of the refrigerator on the third day; the cream suddenly found its way back to the tops of the bottles of milk; and Mohammed, the man with the shop on the corner with the cousin, the one who limped and who had the water buffalo just outside of town, suddenly began to find the fresh buffalo yogurt in the green bowls and was no longer constrained to give us only the factory-made variety.

Men in the neighbourhood began to say hello to William, and the women, whether wearing or not wearing the chador, began to nod and give me peaceful greetings.

Much of my time, however, was still given to my teaching English to Iranian helicopter pilots, which, quite frankly, bored me regardless of how respectful and polite the boys might have been. How many repetitions of 'Good morning, teacher. How are you today?' could the average mind endure? Little did they suspect how vastly different what we taught them was from what they were later to hear from their pilot teachers.

We taught them to say confidently, 'I am preparing for take-off, sir,' while the men who would actually teach them how to handle and control – and fly – a helicopter were far more likely to say, often with a broad Southern accent, 'I'm fixin' for the git-go.' This was often spoken with an accent so thick that I was incapable of understanding it. While we taught them the use of the future tense in sentences like, 'I will try to land to the left of those trees, sir,' our good ole boys told them, 'I'm gonna set this thing down by them trees.'

Over the course of our time together, the students gradually adjusted to the presence of a woman in their classroom, what's more, a woman they had to obey. It was not easy for them, certainly no easier than learning to read in English.

My first month was drawing to an end, and I'd soon be sent back to hearing, 'Good morning, teacher. My name is Hassan.' I spoke to a friend in charge of the Testing Department, who suggested that I transfer there from teaching.

'And do what?' I asked, wondering what fresh hell that would be.

'Play tennis,' he answered.

And so it was. I still took the little yellow American school bus to work every morning, still took the route through the

damaged, rusted, crashed, incinerated, badly landed helicopters parked – though most were simply abandoned – at
the side of the road that crossed the patch of desert on
which the base was built. Now a member of the Testing
Department, at least I no longer had to explain the difference between the present and the past tense. The only way
to speak of these endless lines of abandoned helicopters
was to use the past tense.

Ever punctual, I arrived at work at eight, picked up a
sheaf of papers I'd left on my desk overnight, shook them
a few times, as if checking for insect life, and called across
the room to my superior, 'Pat, I'm just taking these papers
over to Administration.'

Hours later, my tennis partner and I returned and I
did the same things in reverse order, ending by locking
my tennis racquet in my locker. No longer wearing my
tennis whites, I went to my desk and continued with our
major task: convincing both the American and the Iranian
militaries that our statistical, mathematical proof of the
students' verbal ability in English was sufficient reason to
justify the Administration's desire to persist in shovelling
endless millions into the ever-expanding language pro-
gramme. On both sides thus was simple proof suppressed,
and things continued to be fine for everyone.

As time passed, the Administration offices began to
seem to us like Lourdes in the desert. People with prob-
lems, serious or not, had faith that 'Administration' could
resolve all woes, put an end to all turmoil and suffering.

Beg, implore, ask, fall on your knees if you must, but just keep going back: sooner or later, your prayers were sure to be answered. People went there if the spare tyres for the yellow buses failed to arrive. Wait long enough, and they would be found. Praise the Lord. Commissary's run out of kitchen rolls? Be patient, just wait, maybe next week. And then there they were, two planes full of paper products. Praise the Lord.

Those of us who were not heavily burdened by our jobs found ways to fill our days. On Tuesdays, if I recall correctly, we went to the souk to buy fresh vegetables and fruit, and on Thursdays, we went into the bazaar to look at carpets and miniatures.

And each month, the man from Bell Helicopter, our master who lived in the great white palace on Pahlavi Street in Tehran, would appear in our midst and distribute envelopes to us all. Praise the Lord.

Jack and Jill

Hmm, narrative? You want to know about narrative? That's telling a story, isn't it? I remember one of the first I heard, must be seventy years ago, maybe more.

> Jack and Jill went up the hill to fetch a pail of water.
> Jack fell down and broke his crown, and Jill came tumbling after.

That's narrative. Two little kids: Jack and Jill. I assumed they were brother and sister, and that they would be like me. They have a goal: to fill the pail with water. I did not think about why they had to go *up* a hill to fetch water, but I suppose I was too busy with the discovery of words that rhymed to think about such hydrogeological details.

Then we have the crisis, just as we would in Greek tragedy: Jack falls down. Why? He's a kid, so he's not drunk, and there's no mention that anyone's tripped him up or put something in his path – Jack's just a clumsy kid who trips over his own feet. We find out the result of that fall: he breaks his crown (my parents explained that this was his head, else I surely would have gone through life thinking that Jack was really King Jack) and then Jill comes tumbling down the hill after him. She's his sister (remember?), so she's probably just as clumsy as he is.

End of story. Save for motive (was Jack tripped up, and if so, who tripped him?), it's all there: characters, plot, ending. But no motive.

I would guess that, after the third or fourth bottle of wine at a dinner party, some students of lit crit have dedicated themselves to varied analyses of this story. Think of what some critics would do with the fact that Jill is mentioned after Jack and, after his failure, follows him into defeat without attempting to assert herself as an autonomous being, thus perpetuating sexist indoctrination. The Marxists would no doubt point to the inevitability of historical processes that lead to the auto-destruction of crowned heads, those perfidious running dogs of capitalism. One trembles at what the Freudians would get up to with two small children, a deep hole, and a bucket.

But still we have no motive. So although we have characters, a plot, and an ending, we lack what many people think is the most interesting and important element in literature: a reason why everything happens, a motive. And until we have some motivation, we don't have any feelings for the characters, no reason to like or dislike either Jack or Jill or, truth be told, to care much about his crown or his fall, or hers.

Or try these:

He killed his neighbour.

He envied his neighbour.

He liked his neighbour.

He robbed his neighbour.

All of these verbs could initiate interesting narratives, but until a reason for his behaviour is provided, most readers will remain unsatisfied. The narrative can span continents, enter a fifth dimension, go off to other planets, move around in time, but until the reader is told why all of this is going on, he or she is going to be left standing on the edge of the city or the sea or the cosmos, wondering why any of this is happening.

It is hardly my place to tell writers what to do, but I think it is common sense to observe that most people have a natural curiosity about why things happen.

Another element of narrative that is missing from the Saga of Jack and Jill is the judgement of the narrator. This is evident in the complete absence of adjectives and adverbs. No one is giving, or suggesting, an opinion: 'Silly' Jack? 'Careless' Jack? 'Carefree' Jack? 'Generous' Jack? Not a bit of it. 'Poor' Jack fell down? 'Unfortunately' broke his crown? 'Deservedly' broke his crown? And Jill? Was she silly, or loyal, or careless, or brave?

What are we supposed to think about what happens to Jack? Obviously, no one wants to read – at least apart from in religious texts and sermons – anything that commands us how to think. We want the writer to seduce us into thinking a certain way, not poke us with a sharp stick.

In the Saga of Jack and Jill, however, there's not even a whisper or a nudge or a quick glance out of the corner of the writer's eye.

Even Hemingway, famous for his absence from his texts, is always busy nudging us along towards the opinions he wants us to have. There's no question about who's the bad guy in 'Hills Like White Elephants', no matter how hard the voice transmitting that opinion strives towards inaudibility.

As every Border collie knows, you can't herd sheep until they trust you. Same thing with readers: the minute you start to preach to them, they're out the back door of the church, even if it means leaving their hats and bibles in the pew. So a writer has to sneak up on them, stroke their cheeks, use open postures to display honesty and trustworthiness, and then set things up in the story, or the poem, or the novel, or the whatever-it-is, in such a way that the reader is on the slippery slope of trust and agreement. Then set the characters at play and make them *do* things, *say* things that reveal their souls, and perhaps the reader will respond to them, either positively or negatively: it doesn't matter which, really. It's the response that's magic. Strangely enough, it also works at second hand. Where exists the reader of Patrick O'Brian's sea novels who does not venerate Admiral Nelson, although he does not appear as a character in the books, Captain Aubrey worships him, and if he's a hero to the Captain, then by God, he's a hero to us as well.

In a story or a novel, the reader is being persuaded to take sides: good guy, bad guy; good robot, bad robot; good animal, bad animal. This reaction, whether positive or negative, springs from something the writer makes a character say or do; some remark or action that allows the reader to peek into the soul of the character. It is this glimpse of common humanity – or its absence – that is the magic of fiction.

Heroes

Getting Zapped

For some years, I have worked with a baroque orchestra, Il Pomo d'Oro, while at the same time frequently attending baroque operas in many countries. I've also written some short pieces about music, making no attempt to moderate my enthusiasm for the baroque repertory. My enthusiasm for this particular sort of music can be carbon-dated to a performance of Handel's *Alcina* in concert version, at Carnegie Hall, more than fifty years ago. Having once heard, and liked, *Messiah*, I tried an opera: went into the theatre a moderate person, emerged a poor copy of St Paul after his fall from his horse.

Gentle reader, it was not ever so. There was a time when I taught English literature at a private school in Switzerland – one of the good ones – where I tried to interest my students in classical music. Had I tried to interest them in daily prayer meetings, I would have had more success. We stood on opposite sides of the Sound Wall and would surely have spent the entire year separated had not some of the students fallen into a frenzy of love for music manifested in the manner of the early stages of St Vitus' Dance.

Because of my musical ignorance, I did not understand, nor appreciate, the nature of the turmoil until one of
the students sat me down and explained the truth. Frank
Zappa – of whom I had never heard – was to give a concert in the Montreux Casino. This was a chance to hear
and see *Frank Zappa*. 'Oh, please, Miss Leon, would you
come with us as chaperone? If you don't come, we won't
be able to go. And it's FRANK ZAPPA.'

My initial impulse was to decline, then lie, but when
the students failed to find another teacher willing to go,
the stakes rose, and I had to endure signs of Teenage Pain,
Adolescent Sorrow, and Pubescent Disappointment. Like
an overripe plum, I fell.

Two weeks later, I was sitting on the floor of the Montreux Casino, surrounded by teenagers. They were tall;
they were blonde; they were short; they were boys; they
were girls. The only thing they had in common was that
they were all stoned out of their heads, for they had
used their time getting to Montreux or standing in line
for the casino to smoke what they smoked and ingest
what they ingested.

Because I was born in 1942, well before the world-
wide success of drugs, I knew little about them and – I
confess – had never tried any. Nor was I familiar with
the behaviour of people who were using them. In
practical terms, this meant I was sitting on the floor,
surrounded by fifteen teenagers all of whom were in

different psychic conditions. And some of them seemed to believe that they were in different places.

The concert began, if memory serves, in mid-afternoon. There were about four thousand people inside. There were no chairs, so everyone chose to sit on the floor. My students sat bunched together much in the manner of the baby rabbits I used to see on my grandfather's farm. They leaned against one another, sat back to back, arm in arm, rested their heads on the closest knees, and they smiled, models of peaceful humanity.

The music began with what I was told was a 'Warm-Up Band'. Ah, I thought, like the overture to an opera: to set the tone.

Suddenly a tall man with long hair and a lot of facial hair arrived and jumped up onto the stage. Delirium. Or perhaps what comes after delirium. Lots of yelling, a great deal of howling, and then some music, overamplified to a volume that involved pain.

Other men joined him on the stage, adding to the volume of the music and the excitement of most of the audience.

Soon thereafter, I heard a male voice in the audience, speaking English in a tone of wonder and joy, and saying: 'Hey, man, look at that. That's cool, man, cool.' Had he been more than half a metre from me, I surely would not have heard him. Then he said: 'Wow, that's cool. The ceiling, the ceiling.' Well, the music wasn't entertaining me very much, so I thought I'd give the ceiling a try. But it wasn't cool: it was on fire. A small part of the ceiling was burning, and many people were getting to their feet. Then most people were getting to their feet, and the fire was spreading.

Someone – I think it might have been Frank Zappa himself – spoke into a microphone and told the audience the building was on fire and asked them to leave calmly. I went over to my groggy bunnies and asked them to get up because we were leaving. No one protested, no one questioned, nor was there any pushing or shoving or panic. Obviously the drugged state of the audience served them well and probably saved their lives. My bunnies stayed in a thick group and walked quietly towards the exit.

Outside, the building was surrounded by what had just moments before been the audience. Most of them had thought to pick up their jackets and bags, though this in no way slowed things down. Should I ever be in a fire in a public place, please let us all be drugged.

A huge crowd surrounded the burning building and moved further away when the local firefighters arrived in what seemed a very short time. Even this early, it was evident that the fire was out of control. Occasionally, loud explosions sounded inside: there had been an enormous quantity of audio equipment. Each explosion was followed by many cries of 'Wow!' Many were judged to be 'cool'.

I repeatedly counted my bunnies, and finally I lined

them up like kids in kindergarten and told them to take the hand of one other person and not to let it go, not for anything. Linked to one another like this, we watched the building burn to the ground, just as we watched two floor-to-ceiling windows explode outwards, miraculously doing no harm to anyone. I kept patrol of my charges so they didn't turn away or get lost or even lie down.

It was already growing dark when we started to walk, a long line of hand-holding adolescents, moving towards the railway station to go back to school.

We reached it, and I told them they could sit down on a low wall, but they could not let go of their partner's hand.

Sweet reason seemed, very slowly, to be returning to my mind. The kids were safe, they were sitting in front of me, some of them bent over their partner and already asleep. Holding hands, still.

I realized I had the responsibility to call the school – less than an hour had passed – and report that we were all safe. I opened my bag and pulled out a handful of coins while repeatedly reciting the school's main number.

I found a public phone in front of the train station. I picked up the receiver and heard that low hum with which public phones requested you feed them money. And discovered that I didn't recognize the metal thing I was holding in my left hand, nor did I know what I was meant to do with the money in my right hand.

More than forty years after this event, this tale was to propel me into Real Fame. A friend invited me to their family picnic in a small park in South Tyrol. Her teen-age grandson was there, talking to a friend about Deep Purple, which I assumed was the colour of the sweater he was wearing. Not at all: it was a band made famous by yet another song I'd never heard of, 'Smoke on the Water'. When the legendary background of this text was explained to me, I remarked that I had been at that concert.

An ancestor of this family had been a soldier in the First Crusade and had returned safely to their castle in Churburg, wearing his red cross over his padded cloth jacket to indicate his status as a Crusader.

Had he appeared at the picnic at just that moment, per-haps with a jostling trail of armed knights behind him, no one would have given him a second glance, or spoken to any one of them, or made an enquiry about the crosses on their chests. Not when the boys had a famous person to talk to.

Detectives and Villains

My favourite detective hero is Ruth Rendell's Inspector Wexford, and the cause of my enthusiasm is his intelligence and sensibility, both of which, no doubt, mirror his creator's. Further, he's sane: that is, he reflects upon the world and knows his position in it, and his worth. He's a thinker, a man who approaches the world with his mind rather than with his feelings. He's married, loves his wife and his children, and has won my heart by lulling himself to sleep trying to remember the names of the homes in Jane Austen's novels.

Equally humane and sane is Reginald Hill's Fat Andy Dalziel, though one does hope that these two qualities are the only ways in which his creator resembled him. Under a mountain of porcine vulgarity lurks – no doubt to Dalziel's considerable chagrin – a profound compassion for human weakness and human pain, as well as a mind that cuts through sham like a hatchet through lard. Nothing shames him, no words seem sufficient to insult him, yet he is capable of a gossamer delicacy of feeling when necessary – and when he's sure no one's looking. His humour, most often based on the most outrageous sort of disrespect for all the pieties, is bracing in an age of militant political correctness.

Ross Macdonald's Lew Archer started it all, didn't he, with his abiding sympathy for human weakness and his inability to resist a hard-luck story? Like the other two, he is attractive to women sensitive enough to respond to his ethical core; and like Wexford and Dalziel, he becomes one of the Eumenides in his search for the person guilty of the crime. He can also, with one of his sparse metaphors, strip a person or a culture to the bone.

The triviality of my mind is most easily seen in the fact that I persist in reading *Oedipus Rex* as a murder mystery. It's all there: the original crime, off in the distant past; the brooding household and nervous wife; the detective obsessed with revealing the mystery, regardless of what he realizes is mounting danger to himself; and the endless succession of clues, all unravelled by the reader before the detective gets there. Never since has the prevailing metaphor of sight been so vital to the detection of guilt.

My favourite villain is Eunice Parchman in Ruth Rendell's *A Judgement in Stone*, Eunice Parchman 'who killed the Coverdale family because she could not read or write'. Eunice is hateful. She has had a sad, brutal childhood, and she's loathsome. She is much put upon by life, was deprived of all joy in her youth, and she arouses not the least twitter of compassion in the reader. Rendell understands most things better than other writers; the one thing she understands best is evil. She knows it deserves no sympathy and has none for it herself; furthermore she's wise enough to know that good people will never really understand it and ought not bother to try.

Patricia Highsmith's Tom Ripley is another great villain, though where Eunice is sterile and dull, he bursts with life and charm. He's the kind of man you'd like to have a drink with, and while you were at it, he'd have your wallet and then perhaps your life. Most of the monster figures of contemporary crime fiction, the tedious serial killers who can do nothing but chop, chop, chop, are dull to the point of tears because they are so unbelievable, their evil so ungraspable and alien. But Highsmith allows us to sense his charm and, in the process, see the world as he does. It's always made me uncomfortable to suspect that Highsmith saw the world this way, too.

Orlando's a Nutcase

Forgive, please, the lapse into American slang, but the expression 'nutcase' does lie in a dark corner of my vocabulary: what better place to use it than for the main character of the Halle Handel Festival's 2022 production of *Orlando*, in which Ariosto's *Orlando Furioso* comes to the opera stage in a state considerably more advanced than *furioso*?

Orlando, in love with Angelica, is warned by a magician to worry about female treachery. He refuses to believe this is possible until the nose of jealousy slips itself under the flap of his tent and he begins to doubt the fidelity of Angelica, and then the fidelity of all women. Surely he has cause: women don't want to do what he wants them to do. Does a hero need better proof that he has been betrayed and thus has the right to revenge?

Even in the opening scenes of this production, Orlando's behaviour is strange: obsessive bodybuilding, cocktails for breakfast, followed by cocaine. He then flips through his phone, hunting for the photo of the Perfect Woman, as if trying to order her from Amazon.

By the beginning of the second part, he's mad. Perhaps

his suspicions about Angelica's fidelity drive him mad, or perhaps murderous jealousy is the default mechanism for some men. In a 'seduction scene' (or is it Orlando's dream?), he sees Angelica and Dorinda dress themselves in his cliché of female sexuality – bathing suit, cheap robes, and ten-centimetre heels – thus managing to push himself closer to murderous violence.

Over the decades, I've seen various stage productions of *Orlando*: I've seen him committed to psychiatric wards, or suffering from post-traumatic shock in a 1920s veterans' hospital; I've even seen him wandering around, apparently vaguely confused that someone has changed the arrangement of the living-room furniture. But no production has suggested that he was a menace to human life.

Walter Sutcliffe's production in Halle, on the other hand, threw Orlando's madness in our faces. This guy is crazy, but REALLY crazy. If you saw him coming towards you on the sidewalk, glowing under his halo of violence, you'd cross the street. There's the knife and, in case that's not going to do a good enough job, the hammer. This Orlando must have been a brilliant military tactician, for he has thought well ahead and procured some PPC suits, multiple pairs of plastic gloves, gone to the madman's IKEA and brought home all sorts of equipment for imprisoning women: for handcuffing them, hanging them from ropes, disposing of their bodies. He's even dropped in at the local electronics store and picked himself up multiple video screens and a lovely tripod and video camera so that in the future he can spend time looking back and savouring the way he took care of things. Logical, methodical, careful.

Some of the Halle audience thought the production was 'too dark', 'too graphic', 'too real', as though opera were like Caesar's wife, always to be decorous and above suspicion, and anger to be shown by nothing louder than a slightly raised voice. The shocking violence of this production leaves no doubt about the horror of Orlando's madness.

Surely this production will shock and displease those who see opera as the maiden aunt of culture, expected to stand around with folded hands, wearing the outdated stays of propriety, never being so vulgar as to show something that is 'too real'. A reading of the libretto of *Orlando* shows just how 'real' this staging has a right to be. All the horror is in the text: it needs only to be freed by imagination. Yes, it's horrible to watch, eye-coveringly horrible, but it gives the arias of the female singers a meaning and poignancy not given if Orlando does little more than raise his voice and shake his fist.

The title of the poem upon which the opera is based, Aristo's *Orlando Furioso*, describes Orlando: he's *furioso*. He's a warrior: he's hacked people to death. The best thing his friends can do for him is *'fammi combattere'*.

Handel himself, hundreds of years ago, must have felt the cold hand of propriety overhanging his opera, for he chose to end it with the usual *lieto fine*. Peace and friendship are restored, and Orlando can sing, *'Di se stesso e d'amor oggi ha vittoria,'* boasting that he has today 'won victory over love and himself'. As the last notes float away in this production, the audience is left on its own to determine whether his claim is true or not.

String-Pulling in Venice

The Diamond Man

One of the most important parts of a writer's life is the research. This is obviously the case with non-fiction, where the writer plods from fact to fact, and must get them all right: the geography, the laws cited, historical events, battles, the laws of physics and astronomy, and all the carbon dating, including things like the charts of royal families that line up the kings and queens like bowling pins.

Writing fiction demands careful research too. No matter whether it was the butler or the fourth wife who prepared the strychnine-laced hot chocolate for His Lordship to sip at while in his library, the poison has to have no smell (that's cyanide). And it's necessary to put veins and the aorta in the right place before a character slices through one of them.

Google and other sources of 'facts' are sometimes contradictory, or it happens that the sources the writer consults give differing or contrary explanations of an event or a person. (Just think of what you'll encounter that has been written about Karl Marx.)

Blessed, therefore, is the writer who finds a reliable source, a person who is truly expert in a subject and is acknowledged as such by other experts. These are the people who know what wind needs to be blowing to bring the sardines to the surface, when to add cobalt oxide to make glass turn blue, how to judge the age of a painting.

Some years ago, I wrote a book – *Blood from a Stone* – in which 'blood diamonds' or 'combat diamonds' appeared. They were, and still are, mined in places where law has been replaced by greed, always fertile soil in which to plant the seeds of what will grow into a crime story. In these places, hundreds of heavily armed men fight for the possession of diamond mines. Not only diamonds but gold and emeralds and sapphires as well. Much of this is still happening in Africa. In fact, if a map with the locations of these mines were spread out flat on a table and another map showing the locations of small wars were set down over it, many sites would overlap.

To write with the ease and familiarity that suggest complete immersion in this world, no matter how little is finally written, a writer must find the Diamond Man. Or the Chicken Farm Man, or Upton Sinclair's Sausage Man, or just about anyone's Global Warming Man. Bear in mind, please, that the fictional passages that result from conversations with these Men do not have to *be* true: they have only to *sound* true.

A friend of mine who is a jeweller found me my Diamond Man, a quest made easy by the fact that they'd been at school together. He also assured me that Filippo did not deal in blood diamonds. And so, after a few phone calls, Filippo agreed to see me at the place where he did business.

Two days later, I presented myself there, notebook and pencils in my bag, and rang the bell. I was surprised by the door, for it looked like a normal door in a normal home in a normal city, not the salesroom of the most famous diamond dealer in the Veneto.

Suddenly I heard the lock turn. Then I heard another lock turn and another. And then the door opened inwards and I stood facing a man who looked like my uncle. He looked like your uncle. He looked like every uncle I'd ever seen: normal height, thinning grey-brown hair, dark brown eyes, soft, almost timid smile, very nice brown plaid jacket and recently polished brown shoes. He had been blessed with the appearance of kindness.

He stepped back and told me to come in. Saying nothing more, he led me towards the back of the house, past a spotless kitchen and the closed door of what I thought might be the bathroom, and opened what he said was his office, flicking on the light and stepping back to let me enter first.

I saw four chairs, two on each side of a long rectangular wooden table, and what I at first thought was a refrigerator, that steel-doored SUV of refrigerators seen in American kitchens. It proved, however, to be a safe. There were the two round metal knobs that are always twirled and manage to open such safes just as the bad guys leap in through the windows and tell people to lie on the floor.

Filippo instead asked me if I'd like a coffee; I declined.
I tried to look uninterested, if only to assure him that I had
nothing at all to do with whoever might be standing outside and preparing to jump in with a machine gun in his
hands. I relaxed a bit and looked around the room. There
were no paintings, no lamps save the very bright one in
the ceiling above the table, no anything.

'Lino told me you were interested in diamonds,' Filippo began and then smiled. 'I know you're here for
information . . . not for buying.'

Thus began my class in diamonds. I'd already read
about the source of the stones, the often mile-deep crev-
ices in the earth, called pipes, where they were trapped,
sometimes for hundreds of millions of years, until some
motion in the pipe sets them working upwards. And I'd
learned where most were found: apart from Africa, in
Russia, Canada and Australia.

After that, Filippo told me of the quantities that
were found, where the cutting was done, how it could
take years for cutters to decide how best to cut a stone.
The longer he spoke, the more his passion became audible and visible.

'Let me show you some,' he said, and turned to the
safe. I moved my chair sideways to be sure his body
blocked any chance I had to follow his hands when he
opened the safe. I folded my notebook back to the beginning and turned away to read what I'd written so far.

I heard a flopping noise and he said, laughing, 'You can come back now.'

I turned around and saw on the desk between us a black velvet wallet the size of a kitchen napkin. Filippo opened the two flaps, pressed them flat on the table, and pulled seven or eight small, transparent Ziploc bags from the horizontal slots in the sides. The bags were no bigger than the size of a pack of cigarettes; some were smaller. Each bag held one stone only. He opened a drawer in the desk and pulled out a black velvet cloth the same size as the wallet, which he snapped open, lay on the table, and smoothed flat with his open palms. He studied the small bags on the table in front of him, selected three, opened them one by one, rolled the diamonds on the cloth, and told me to look at each one carefully and tell him if I saw any sign of colour.

I grabbed the side panels of my chair from underneath and leaned forward. 'No colour?' I asked, freeing my hand to point to the one furthest to the left. 'That one?'

He nodded and asked, 'The next?'

Without hesitation, the answer was there. 'Blue, but only if it's possible,' I said after leaning closer to the stone.

He nodded and asked, 'The last one?'

'Green?'

'No. It's another blue.'

'Did you choose the most obvious ones?' I asked him.

'Yes.'

'Two out of three,' I said.

'Not bad.'

I leaned back in my chair and put my hands in my lap. Filippo scooped the three stones back into their separate bags, zipped them closed, and slipped them back into their slots, then reached for others.

For the next half hour, he showed me the jewels in his crown – if you will permit me to use that phrase. He rolled them out, one by one, careful to move them around only with the point of a leadless mechanical pencil he pulled from the inside pocket of his jacket.

Only once did he make a reference to their value, when he slid four diamonds from separate bags and lined them up in a row.

'Which do you think is the most valuable?' he asked, passing me the pencil so I could turn them over or around if I chose to. I turned them all a bit to the right, but they still looked as they had, all the same.

I passed him back the pencil, smiling. 'I've no idea,' I finally said.

He started to push them back, one by one, into their bags. When they were all safely inside, he asked, eyes on the diamonds, 'What do you think the difference is between the least and the most valuable?'

I looked down at them again, safe in their transparent garages, but still they all looked the same.

'I've no idea,' I finally answered.

'Do you want to guess which they are? And how big

the difference is?' he asked, then smiled, as if that would help reveal the trick to the question.

'I don't want to know,' I said. 'But I think you want to tell me.'

He laughed so loudly I thought the diamonds would fall off the table.

'Perhaps' was his cryptic response.

He showed me many more, but then I saw that I'd been there almost two hours and had surely outstayed my welcome. I closed my notebook and moved back in my chair, told him I believed I'd got some understanding of diamonds and feeling for them, which might even have been the truth.

I thanked him and offered my hand across the table. I was exhausted. 'I don't know how to thank you, Filippo,' I said, suddenly conscious of the fact that I had been speaking to him in the familiar '*tu*', something I was not at all accustomed to doing with people I met for the first time.

'The pleasure was entirely mine,' he said, getting to his feet. He turned back to the safe, closed both doors, then spun the knobs, seeming to enjoy that part of the ritual. Then, either reluctantly or sadly, he said, 'I seldom get asked anything about diamonds other than the price.' And then, sounding even sadder, 'Even my son – it's all he asks about. He isn't interested in them, just what they cost.'

'So what will happen to all of this?' I took the liberty of asking, nodding towards the safe.

He shrugged. 'I suppose he'll sell them all. He's never loved them the way I do.'

'I'm sorry' was the only thing I could think of to say.

'It's what happens,' he said, trying to make it sound like it didn't really matter very much.

I nodded and started towards the corridor. He came behind me and went with me to the door to the street.

'It was a great pleasure,' I said. And then, to please him, 'I had no idea they were so beautiful.'

'Oh, they are.'

Filippo worked his way down the locks and opened the door.

I put out my hand again and repeated my thanks.

We shook hands, and I resisted the impulse to kiss him on both cheeks. I took a few steps in the direction of the vaporetto, then turned back at the first corner and waved, but he had already gone into the house.

Two years later, Filippo fell victim to two men, skilled jewel thieves, who spent months grooming him to be robbed, beginning with the fake coincidence of meeting his wife on a train. Posing as diamond dealers and demonstrating extraordinary knowledge and taste, they persuaded him to show them the best pieces he had for sale. Because he'd come to trust them, he showed them the same black wallet on different occasions. He believed their compliments about his taste and judgement.

On their last visit – at least this is what I was told – they distracted him for the half second that allowed them to switch his black wallet with a facsimile and leave with the diamonds, which were never recovered.

A year later, he died. I never learned the cause. Italian law sees that the family inherits, so I assume that his son became the owner of any remaining diamonds. I never tried to find out anything more.

Venice 1729

The origins of Carnevale lie thousands of years in the past, in festivities meant to turn society topsy-turvy by releasing a social and behavioural safety valve. The Romans celebrated Saturnalia – the feast of the god Saturn – just before the winter solstice. It provided people with a bit of joy, pleasure, and overeating to help them through the coming winter months. Slaves and masters temporarily changed places: the master waited on his slaves at table, while the slaves could ignore him or tell him what to do. Furthermore, there was a certain measure of sexual misbehaviour and normal urban life was disrupted.

Christianity picked up the custom, without the sex, and thus the period before the beginning of Lent, with its many renunciations, became a time of similar excess, especially in Venice, that painted whore of cities. During the period of Carnevale, masters and servants wore the same clothing and became indistinguishable when wearing the same masks, and thus each was free to behave in the manner of the other class. Women, too, were masked, so there was no telling whose husband walked arm in arm with whose wife.

Venice 1729

Venice took to Carnevale with a passion. It expanded until society stopped counting the days, by which time it lasted almost half the year. Carnevale thus accelerated a tendency towards social equality that already existed in Venetian society, where workmen could live in the house next door to a count and countess, and the non-noble merchant class held a great deal of power. After all, the city described itself as a republic. And now those troublesome masks enforced the idea that people were somehow equal. Even worse, people wearing them were suddenly anonymous. By 1592, those wicked masks were being accused of leading to 'dissolution, fraud, dishonesty, filth, homicide, and treason'.

Which art would lend itself better to this atmosphere of ambiguity, excess, and confusion than opera? Women sang the parts of men, fire-snorting dragons pulled chariots onto the stage, castrated men sang with artificially high voices, and all of Europe flocked to Venice to hear them do it. Everything about opera had something of the carnival spirit in it: princes disguised as beggars, beggars revealed to be princes, women offered the choice between a sword or a cup of poison as a means of death – stories so wonderful they were not to be seen again until television soap opera. Not surprisingly, opera soon became one of the great manifestations of the carnival spirit: costumes, masks, long, dark cloaks, people disguised as what they were not, often doing what they should not. And just think, they sang while all this was going on.

There was more of that dangerous republican spirit in the way operas were presented in Venice. They were not performed by a company maintained by a music-loving prince or princeling, where attendance was by invitation only. Instead, maintaining the entrepreneurial spirit of Venice, theatres were built all over the city by private owners, and tickets were sold to anyone who had the money to pay for them. Thus was created the perfect symbiosis between art and commerce.

Not only did opera in Venice encourage dangerous republicanism: it also led to sexual excess. For in the theatres of Venice there were private boxes in which men and women could sit together, or perhaps, some said, do other things together. You'll be relieved to learn that in other decent, God-fearing countries, such shocking promiscuity was not permitted.

Soon Europe was flooding towards Venice because of the madness of, and the madness for, Carnevale and its most fantastic manifestation, opera. One example is the prince-elector of Hanover who closed up shop for months while he took his court to Venice, where he maintained a palazzo all year round so as to be able to go to the opera during the ever-lengthening period of Carnevale. He found it easy to attend the opera because this city of 140,000 people had at least ten opera houses. The audience was large and passionate, always wanting new operas, new music, and stars, stars, stars.

The year 1729 was to be Venice's most spectacular

carnival opera season. Ever. There were to be seven premieres of operas by some of the greatest composers of the time, and they were to be sung by some of the most famous singers. Among the stars were Farinelli, the most famous castrato of the age, and his chief rival, Senesino. Another star was Faustina Bordoni, the most famous mezzo-soprano. There were also many now-forgotten singers, among them Nicolini and Annibaldi, the castratos, and perhaps Maria Caterina Negri, who would go on to create many contralto roles for Handel. Further, the operas were written by the A list of composers: Porpora, Vinci, Orlandini, Gasparini, Leo, Giacomelli, Albinoni, all of whose operas are now being rediscovered and performed.

But wait a minute, isn't there a name missing here? Where is the greatest opera composer of the time? Where is Handel? Twenty years before, he'd had a sensational Venetian Carnevale debut with *Agrippina* and was now internationally famous as an opera composer. After his Italian triumphs, he'd gone to London and set up his own opera company, but he'd been ruined financially, he claimed, by the greed of his star singers, who had abandoned him when he refused to meet their salary demands. Senesino and Faustina Bordoni had left his foundering Royal Academy of Music for the higher salaries offered in Venice, and his great soprano, Francesca Cuzzoni, had gone to sing in Vienna.

So here we are, in Venice, in the late winter of 1729, about to listen to the music of the greatest composers of the era – minus Number One – and the greatest singers – Minus One. During the entire period of this most spectacular Carnevale, not a note of Handel's music was played or heard. But he was there! Not as a composer but as a headhunter, hoping to lure his great singers back to his theatre in London or, failing that, to pick up new talent. He was there also as a kind of musical magpie, looking for anything shiny and bright and beautiful – a voice, a libretto, or a tune – to take back to London with him.

Handel might have been musically absent from the Carnevale, but his work as an impresario continued: in this pre-copyright era, he was after libretti and arias. When he returned to London, he took for his pasticcio *Catone* the overture and nine arias from Leo's *Catone in Utica* and also inserted arias by Hasse, Vivaldi, Porpora and Vinci. Musicologists argue heatedly about what are generously called Handel's 'borrowings', a pleasant name for copy and paste, which is in itself a pleasant name for theft. He did at least borrow widely from himself, not just from other composers. Borrowing was the custom of the time, made easier by the fact that live performance was the only way most people heard music: the audience forgot the music; musicians remembered.

What was a composer to do if he heard his music appear in another composer's opera? Call his lawyer? Handel owned a copy of the score of Orlandini's *Adelaide*, and when he returned to London, he quickly changed the names of the characters and, keeping substantially to the same story, turned it into his own opera, *Lotario*. Handel also borrowed Porpora's *Semiramide* and presented his own opera in 1733, but this time he stole – er, he borrowed – the music not from Porpora but from Vinci.

This certainly provides evidence that Handel was in Venice to work. To go to the operas, certainly, but to take away with him far more than the memory of the music and the singing. He was there to check out what the other guys were up to. Here was his chance to listen to and pay close attention to the music of most of his rivals, who were presumably at their best, because this was the festival of festivals, where reputations were sure to rise or fall. He was there, and musical souvenirs were all around him free for the taking.

Stories that have come down in letters and diaries suggest that some of the composers were not on the best of terms with others, nor with the singers. I have no idea if this is because of the 'borrowing' but there is frequent mention of dislike and rivalry. Indeed, it was reported that Vinci paid a castrato to sabotage the dress rehearsal of an opera by Porpora. Senesino, loved by all, wrote of a soprano with whom he had sung and described her as 'this woman whom my delicacy is still unable to digest'. Well, I was once present at a recording when a soprano, unable to sing the coloratura written for her by the conductor, shouted, '*Scheiss Variationen*' as she walked out of the room. It's all part of show business, boys and girls.

Almost three hundred years later, does it matter who

stole what from whom? Today we are so accustomed to being able to buy music – as opposed to buying a ticket to a performance – that we forget recorded music is a relatively modern development. Before the phonograph, and now the iPhone, you heard it played live, or you didn't hear it. Perhaps this ephemeral quality made people less concerned with who owned the music or had the rights to perform it. Apparently, they acted upon the belief that once it had been performed, it belonged to anyone who had heard it and had the ability to remember it or the means to write it down.

With a View of San Marco

Some years ago, in late summer, I moved into a new apartment in Venice: top floor, view of San Marco, four skylights, plenty of room. In short, perfection. At least it was until the third night I slept there, when I was catapulted out of a deep sleep by a pistol shot. Stunned, awake, I lay in bed and listened for the sound of running feet; instead, I heard the sound of a car careening away at high speed. Pistol shots are rare in Venice, high-speed car chases rarer still. The answer was as obvious as it was audible: television. I got out of bed, went into the living room, and studied the houses opposite. All were clothed in shuttered sleep, save for the one window from which emerged the telltale grey flickering of a television. Keeping pace with it were the sounds of the growing disaster: crashes, cries, shouts, more shots, and, finally, silence. But not for long, as the film still had an hour to run.

I closed my windows, lay in a room so hot it could have been in Sumatra, got up and opened my windows, but by then the characters in the film across the *campo* were shouting at one another on the telephone. Finally, at about three, admitting defeat, I went and spent the rest of the night in the guest room.

That night set the pace for the summer. I came to know the woman in the window, was told by neighbours that she was a retired teacher in her late seventies, mean as a snake, who had terrorized the neighbourhood for years with her night-time television. Twice during the next few months, I went to the window late at night and shouted across the sleeping *campo*: 'Are we deaf around here?' Once, late in August, at about two in the morning, I got my opera glasses to see what she was up to and saw her, naked as a jaybird, standing at her kitchen sink, drinking a glass of water. I covered my eyes and retreated to the guest room. Two months later, the noise so loud it came through my double-glazed windows, I dared to look again and saw her sound asleep in her bed, facing the larger and louder television in the bedroom.

I called the police, but they said that, alas, there was nothing they could do: the health service might come and measure the decibels of her noise, but there was no way to force her to lower the volume. They were as apologetic as they were useless. Maddened by this, I began to plan. I learned her name, found her doorbell, studied it one day, and realized that by carefully wedging a wooden tooth-pick into it, I could make it ring endlessly, perhaps luring her down the darkened stairs at three in the morning. There was scaffolding on the house next to hers: a friend volunteered to slip onto her roof one night and clip her

antenna cable with his wire cutters. I thought of a sling-
shot: not stones, but ripe figs, tomatoes. I fantasized about
the sudden slap of them against her windows as she slept.
Terrible things have been known to happen to old people
who are suddenly roused from deep sleep by tomatoes.
All winter and spring, as the noise came through her
closed windows, across the *campo*, through my windows
and into my dreams as a dull throb, my battle preparations
grew more sophisticated, more violent.

Once, as I sat trying to read, a series of pistol shots
came across to me. Maddened, I grabbed the phone and
called. I knew her number because I'd planned to harass
her, have my friends in New York call her at 3 a.m. Italian time.

'*Pronto*,' she said.

'*Buon giorno, Signora*,' said I.

'Who is this?'

'A neighbour, Signora.'

'What do you want?'

'I'm sorry to trouble you, Signora, but I've got a sick
person here in my house who is trying to sleep. I wonder
if I could most politely ask you to close your window
a little bit or perhaps minimally lower the sound of the
television.'

She replaced the phone, and a moment later the sound
of the television was lowered. Her compliance both
shamed and surprised me, and I spent the rest of the day
in silent repentance for the violence of my thoughts.

BACKSTAGE

Two days later, at about midnight, what sounded like attack helicopters strafed my windows. I tried the phone, but she'd taken it off the hook, so I moved into the guest room. The next morning, I bought a box of toothpicks.

Redentore

I've long been of a mind that life is, like it or not, a billiard ball: we might start it on its way, but once it gets
moving, it bangs into things we didn't notice and then
takes off in an entirely new direction. So it was with the
Feast of Redentore, that peculiarly Venetian concession
to excess: twenty minutes of fireworks, on a usually
cloudless July night, out over the Bacino di San Marco,
the bell tower diminished to a mere background for the
highest and wildest of them. After the grand finale, the
Marangona sounds out midnight and the hundred thousand people – in recent years – who have come to see
them cheer themselves silly with sheer childlike delight
in bright lights and loud bangs.

It was the one night I insisted on being in Venice – yes,
for the bright lights and the loud bangs. I've seen them
from the Giudecca side, from the San Marco side, from
windows, the water, *altane*, and terraces, and the thought
of watching them reduces me to a quivering jelly of antici-
patory joy.

But I have not seen them for years. The billiard ball is
an old friend, Ada Pesch, leader and founding member

of La Scintilla, the baroque orchestra of the Zurich Opera, who asked me, years ago, if I'd help to create interest in a summer festival in Ernen of which she was the artistic director. She wanted to add a week of baroque vocal music to it and thought the festival would appeal to a wider selection of people if I would volunteer to teach a week-long course in how to write a crime novel.

Without hesitation and with delight and enthusiasm, I agreed, and that's when Ada hit me over the head with the billiard cue, in this case the date of the opening: the Saturday of Redentore. No more fireworks, no more bright flashes and heavy booms, no more midnight ringing of the bells. Instead, baroque opera arias and little-known instrumental pieces performed by Baroque specialists and singers in the selection of whom I'd have a say.

I agreed to give it a try for one year, and here I am, many years later, Redentore-deprived but convinced that the trade was both wise and enjoyable.

The first year, I got an early-morning train on the day of Redentore, just as the city was beginning to fill with the tens of thousands who were coming for the fireworks. The trip took only a little more than five hours, and twenty minutes after arriving in Brig, I was there, at first feeling a little like someone who stumbled down Alice's rabbit hole and awoke to find herself in a postcard.

There were the usual lush green slopes covered with the still-uncut grass of summer. Here and there, I saw goats attempting to chew their way to the other side of the field, although the grass looked so healthy, it would surely grow back in ten minutes. There were a few charmingly posed donkeys, a couple of horses, and then, there they were: cows. Granddaughter of a German dairy farmer, I am particularly subject to the beauty and charm of cows, for, like Konrad Lorenz's geese with him, I bonded with them as a child. Their noses are velvet, and to have them lick the salt from my arm with their Velcro tongues still gives me a surge of joy.

And there they were, dappled brown and white, bells clanging away as they grazed, beginning that magical process, that miracle of nature, by which grass goes in and milk comes out. These are the Swiss kind of cow and – no matter how often or fervently my Swiss friends insist that this is not true – I thus choose to believe that milk goes in and Swiss chocolate comes out.

My chalet had a view down the valley – church tower to the right, snow-capped mountains behind – and, from the bedroom window, of a manicured garden larger than the apartment I had left behind in Venice. Behind the garden stood the church below the tower, where the concerts would be held.

That evening, I met the students, though it's ridiculous to call them that since many of them were my age, some older, and most of them well read and intellectually sophisticated. There was, from the beginning, a sense of mutuality among us. None of this 'Ms Leon' nonsense. I was Donna, and they all had first names, even the oldest of them. And no nonsense about being an expert: I'd simply done one thing a number of times and wanted to explain to them some of the things I'd learned while doing it, hoping that this would make them more acute readers of crime books, and for those interested in trying to write one, to give them an idea of some of the ways to save time and avoid errors.

As an example, I told them that the most important decision they had to deal with before they got on with the plot was to decide who the narrative voice would belong to: a character in the book who would be 'I', or perhaps a narrator who sees things from the point of view of one of the characters, or perhaps a narrator with the gift of omniscience. Furthermore, before making that choice, they had to consider the sex, age, level of culture, sense of humour, and the general spirit of their narrator. Changing sex is easy; changing the level of culture is not. Try it: we all have some idea of how men think, since men run the world and literature is filled with male characters. But we also know how women think because fiction is crowded with female characters who have been revealed to us. But how does the cleaning woman think, or the professor of physics?

One of the great pleasures of those first classes/ encounters with this initial group of students was discovering how widely they had read and how broad was their range of reference. All of them were at least bilingual: we were doing this in English, after all, and only two of them were native speakers of the language. They had thus read the European classics I'd been constrained to read in English, and many of them had the exquisite feel for poetry that comes only with reading it in the language in which it was written.

Not only did they ask questions, they doubted. Even better, their uncertainties and reservations about some of the opinions I or their colleagues expressed about books led to heated discussion. 'How can you read such junk?' someone felt easy enough to ask by the second day.

Halfway through the class, the Ernen feeling (for want of a better word) had already been formed: we were a group of people who loved books, loved reading, and thought that books were vitally important to the running of a happy life, and we had come together to talk about a specific book (that year it was Ruth Rendell's *A Judgement in Stone*, which I still consider one of the best crime books ever written) and from that book make references or comparisons to others. No one imposed a limit on what could be brought into the discussion, so long as the person bringing it could make us see how their comment was relevant to the text.

This pattern has continued through the years: people who love reading come to Ernen for a week to talk about books such as *The House of Mirth, Pride and Prejudice, Jane Eyre*. Furthermore, many of the people who come back to talk about them are recidivists: there is still a group of ten or so who were at the first class, and most of the people who come have been there a number of times. So, in some ways, it has turned into a group of friends who meet to talk about books.

One change is the addition, over the years, of a second bookish type to add variety to the comments and perspectives on the business of writing. To date, the others who have come are Richard Powers, the award-winning American novelist, Tom Holland, a gifted writer of popular history and translator from Latin and Greek, Judith Flanders, a much-acclaimed British social historian, Elisabeth Bronfen, a scholar and writer, and Ravi Mirchandani, a British publisher. Yes, all are friends of mine, people whose judgement about books I trust absolutely. We'd talk about books in other places, so why not do it in Ernen and get to see the cows?

Musically, as well, every year has more than satisfied my disgruntled longing for Redentore. The Ernen Baroque Orchestra, led by Ada Pesch, plays with the same ease and familiarity with which we bookish types speak of literature. They, too, have bonded and see Ernen as a rare opportunity to come together with friends to engage in the thing they love. Because Ada shares my addiction to the vocal music of Handel, his arias have a habit of slipping into the programmes, and many well-known artists have come to sing them: Anna Bonitatibus, Karina Gauvin and Ann Hallenberg.

The festival, under the direction of its intendant, Francesco Walter, is beginning to attract great attention. In

2013, it received the Prix Montagne, and every year the international press grows increasingly enthusiastic about the high quality of its musical performances.

Each year, the first meeting is on the Saturday evening before the class begins, and each year it is a meeting between old friends who use the first hours to catch up: 'How wonderful to see you again.' 'Where have you been?' 'What have you read?'

And then we have an entire week to find out the answers to those questions.

Mortal Danger

Getting Out

During the summer of 1978, William, who had been a Peace Corps volunteer in Iran and spoke perfect Farsi, began to mention the Ayatollah Khomeini and said often that he was worried about the future of Iran because of what he had heard the Ayatollah say on the radio. Within months, William was proven right, for the followers of the Ayatollah did indeed begin the revolution that very quickly put an end to the reign of the Shah, who fled the country in January 1979, introducing an entirely new form of government.

After His Majesty fled the country – he was rumoured to have filled his plane not only with his family but with the crown jewels and a large sum of money – the new government announced that the work contracts of all foreigners were cancelled, though the newly unemployed foreigners were to be allowed to remain in the country if they chose.

I did not choose. Nor did I choose the resulting unemployment. But until the situation became clear, there were tanks in the streets, a six o'clock curfew, and no answers to be had anywhere. Or rather, there were many answers and a great deal of information, but no certainty that any of it was reliable. The American radio warned us about the 'fierce anti-American feeling' that was beginning to manifest itself in the city, indeed, in the entire country. We were told to remain in our houses.

From different official sources, we learned that we could/could not go to Tehran. Our company would/would not pay for our flight from Tehran. The American embassy in Tehran was/was not answering its phone. Foreigners were/were not in danger.

Reality broke through to us one evening when we were listening to the radio and Farsi-speaking William was trying to decipher the message. The Ayatollah gave his opinion on many subjects, none of them very encouraging to the likes of us. Then above the low buzz of radio static sounded three quite moderate knocks on the door to the narrow lane on which we lived. I froze. He froze. We froze. He went to open the door, and I remembered something I had once read about the Russian composer Dmitri Shostakovich: he had always kept a packed suitcase beside the door of his apartment in Moscow and thus thought himself ready for the night-time knock at the door that would come once Stalin was displeased with something he wrote.

The knock was not repeated more harshly, no one banged an angry fist at the door, combat boots did not kick it in. Instead, when we opened it, we saw it was our next-door neighbour, a short woman with light eyes who had always said hello and bowed to us, a sound and a gesture we'd learned to return with even greater seriousness.

Pulling the edge of her chador across the bottom half of her face, leaving only her eyes, she bowed and said, *'Salam aleikum,'* which we both repeated. She then turned to William, though she was careful to stand beside, and a little behind, me. William took a step away from her and looked at the ground. She spoke, he spoke, she spoke and gestured towards her house. He spoke, placed his palms flat upon his chest in a prayerful gesture, and bowed his head. I imitated his gesture. She whispered something and backed into the street, closing the door behind her.

'What did she say?'

'That there's a rumour. She doesn't know if it's true or not, but people are saying the water is poisoned.'

There was nothing I could say, was there?

'But they have a well,' he went on. 'And she says we should go to them for water.'

Like dogs whose masters had died, we continued to go outside the city to the base where we had worked to wait and see what was/was not happening. After a few weeks, during which the possibility of civil war grew undeniable, we were taken to our homes, told to pack two suitcases, and were given two hours to do so.

Exactly on time, our beloved yellow school bus arrived and took us – no, not to the Isfahan airport, but to the still-unfinished model city that was being built to house foreign workers. Giant washing machines and dryers (yes), swimming pool, enormous ovens, tennis courts, air conditioning, attached garages. Close your eyes and you were in Southern California. But with machine-gun fire from the city.

'Take whatever house you prefer,' a very polite Bell Helicopter employee told us. And we did.

It was too far to go to the military base every day, so we settled into our own little San Diego and tried to find a lifestyle. We could sit by the pool and read, save that it was February and the pool was empty. We could stay inside and watch television, but few of us spoke Farsi, and most of the channels were now showing twenty-four-hour prayers.

We played more tennis, a generous soul passed on to me her copy of *The Portrait of a Lady*, allowing me to sit the game out for a day or two. But then it came, the order to leave. One afternoon, my serve was broken by the arrival of a tall, thickset man who still wore the Bell Helicopter uniform. He smiled and said, 'We'll be back in the yeller bus tonight. 'Bout ten. Y'all be ready, hear?' Yellow bus, yeller bus: it was all the same to us, sufficient that it arrive. And leave.

Getting by car from Isfahan to Tehran, regardless of the time of day one was travelling, had always been to flirt with death. The drivers – if I might call them that – had little – er – training or experience, but in the years leading up to these events, countless thousands of Iranians had been able to buy their first car, the affordable Paykan.

After the First World War, a popular song was entitled 'How Ya Gonna Keep 'Em Down on the Farm After They've Seen Paree?' Similarly, how you gonna keep them down on the farm after they've driven a Paykan? Yet someone who knows only the Paykan will most likely drive it as he did the donkey or the horse. The metal roadkill on either side of the highway between the two cities was revelatory, with its suggestion that someone's – perhaps not Napoleon's – army had passed through recently, leaving wreckage on either side: abandoned tyres, hubcaps, car doors, and fenders. There were not only cars but buses and trucks. Very few bicycles, and then only if they had been crushed beyond easy recognition. There were even tractors, although there was no arable land to be seen.

And us, teachers of English as a foreign language who had chosen early retirement, all packed into a mini-caravan of four little American-made Blue Bird school buses, manufactured in the state of Georgia. No, not the one in Europe; the one stuck between South Carolina and Florida. Is it possible to feel sorry for a state?

Before we started for Tehran, I, for some reason, thought that all the traffic would be heading there, probably because from the north of the country it might be possible to reach the Turkish border. It did not seem quite as wise to head in the direction of some of the other neighbouring countries. The thousands of oncoming headlights proved that theory wrong: people were fleeing in both directions. The Iranian bus driver said he had been told to take us to the Inter-continental Hotel.

As a friendly farewell gift to us, he had brought along his Sony cassette player as well as his own collection of tapes, all sung by Googoosh, the most famous singer in Iran – understandably – and he continued to play her classics. The song he played most often was her latest hit, '*Ageh Bemooni*'. When we learned that the title when translated into English meant, 'If You Stay', I did begin to wonder where the driver's loyalties lay.

I rejected the idea of following up that question and kept my attention on Googoosh, whom we'd all been listening to for years. Her voice had come to us from everywhere: over the walls of houses, from cars stopped at red lights, from transistor radios carried at all times. In our little yellow bus, we heard the same slow undulation of the theme, and then the voice was suddenly there: sweet, perhaps oversweet to a Western ear. But the Western ears were leaving, weren't they? Some took with them the memory of those undulant rhythms, the winds and light hand drums, and that sweet, sweet voice. The next song was my favourite, '*Bavar Kon*', and to hear it again today on YouTube is to have the softness and grace of life brought back. Memory also brings those elegantly courteous people, those builders of Persepolis. Occasionally, I listen to her on YouTube, and each time

I do, I check to see how long it has been since the last listener was moved enough by her music to leave a comment. Not too long ago, I was saddened to see it was seven years since the last comment, but the last time I checked, it was only a month. Googoosh lives!

Sleep took Googoosh from us, and we woke to the sight of the Inter-Continental Hotel: twelve floors, tanks pulled up around it. There was no way of knowing who was holding up his hand to us; we obeyed only the gestures made by a weapon. Most of the men milling around the hotel wore combat fatigues, but that didn't mean much since it hadn't been decided which side was represented by which uniform. Whom were they loyal to? Fighting for? Willing to die for? Kill for? Most had, at best, half a uniform and half a notion.

A desk had been set up at the entrance to the hotel; behind it sat a bearded young man, his hands folded on a pile of papers. Our driver explained who his passengers were, and the bearded man removed his hands from the papers and started to flip through them. We whispered to one another not to speak.

The driver asked for our passports: we handed them over with no protest; he gave them to the other man. The young man asked a question, and the driver answered, speaking for some time. The young man handed him some papers, then gave the driver our passports and refolded his hands on the remaining papers.

The driver led us back to the bus and returned our passports. Then he went through the papers in his hand, quite a thick pile, and explained that when we received ours, we were to check a room key was taped to the front. That was the room we were to use until the next day: our flight left at ten in the morning and would take us to Frankfurt.

One of the American helicopter pilots I'd known in Isfahan appeared – he'd been on a different bus – and after I found my key, he offered to carry my suitcase up to the seventh floor for me. When we got there, he took my key and opened the door to the room, closed it behind us and told me not to move. He crouched down and shuffled over to the shattered windows and pulled the curtains closed, cutting off most of the light in the room. Behind him, the remaining light created a wild non-pattern of cracks and holes as it came through the gap in the curtains. Large pieces of glass had fallen to the floor. I glanced around, and it wasn't until then that I noticed the holes in all the walls.

'Boys with guns,' he said, then, 'Don't take your shoes off.' A moment's thought and then he added, 'And sleep in the bathtub, not the bed.'

He looked at his watch, and I looked at mine. It was already five in the afternoon, and the first signs of twilight were sneaking towards us. I took a step closer to the window, curious about Tehran by night.

82

He put a hand on my arm and said, 'Don't walk in front of the window, and keep the curtains closed even when it's dark. Put one of the bedside lamps on the floor to use for light, if you have to.' He walked over to the door, put the key in the lock, turned to repeat, 'Don't go near the windows,' and left.

In the distance, muted sounds began. *Hummm, hummmm.* They continued for a bit. It grew darker. The sounds stopped after a while, but after some time, they were replaced by zip zip zip volleys that went on for a long time.

I put my suitcase on the floor by the door and took out a package of dates, a brown paper bag with a kilo of pistachio nuts, and a large plastic bottle of water I'd drawn from the kitchen sink late the previous afternoon.

Behind the closed curtains, I set the chair next to the gap where the two sides of the curtain met. I sat and gave the night all the time it needed to take over, both outside and inside the room.

I opened the curtain about the width of my thumb and scooched the chair closer. There was Tehran, the two other hotels, cars, some with and some without their lights.

Occasionally there were loud booms; sometimes there were short-lived bursts of zip zip zip. I ate the dates slowly, perhaps ten of them, and then I ate a handful of the pistachios. I was careful to see that the date pits, dark and sticky with sugar, went into the waste-paper basket, but I was less careful with the pistachios, and some of the shells fell on the floor. I left them: I was wearing my shoes, after all.

When it was fully dark, I locked the door to the room, trying to ignore the bullet holes, went to the closet and pulled down two blankets. The light in the bathroom still worked, but I was careful and turned it on only when I was inside. The water ran, so I washed my hands and face, brushed my teeth like a good girl, but drank the water from the bottle, not the tap. One never knows.

I spread the blankets on the bottom of the bathtub and went back into the room to get a pillow, but the same glass that had fallen on the bed was also on the pillows. I went over to the curtains, broadened the space between the two sides a bit more, and looked down at Tehran, capital of the Empire of Persia, home of King Mohammad Reza Pahlavi, Light of the Aryans, Grand Collar of the Order of Pahlavi, Sovereign of the Order of Zolfaghar, Knight Grand Cordon of the Order of the Crown, Sovereign of the Order of the Red Lion and the Sun, Sovereign of the Order of Splendour, Sovereign recipient of the Scout Medal.

> And on the pedestal, these words appear:
> 'My Name is Ozymandias, king of kings:
> Look on my works, ye Mighty, and despair!'
> Nothing beside remains. Round the decay
> Of that colossal wreck, boundless and bare
> The lone and level sands stretch far away.

Great Expectations

One book that I keep returning to is Dickens's *Great Expectations*, which I fell in love with when I was fifteen. It's a book about growing up that tells the story of Pip, a poor orphan apprenticed to a blacksmith, who is chosen by an anonymous benefactor and sent from the countryside to London, where he is to be transformed. We watch him become a man, a gentleman, and finally a decent man.

I read it first as I read most of Dickens's books for the first time: for the sheer genius and invention of the plot, for all those bizarre minor characters, for the bad people who were oh, so very bad. Even then, however, I was struck by the absence of what many of his other novels provide and what I suppose I was anticipating: a happy ending. Yes, it's there, the happy ending – boy gets girl – but that's only because he changed his original ending, in which the boy did not get the girl and was lucky not to get her.

Oh, there are weird characters in abundance, and who weirder than Miss Havisham, sitting near the spiderweb-covered corpse of her wedding cake and her hopes? And there's the young Estella, even then a beauty, who indeed becomes the Star of all Pip's hopes – Estella, raised to make men suffer.

There are also the minor characters, each separate and distinct and each a bit strange: Wemmick the clerk and Magwitch the convict, Herbert Pocket, Pip's dearest friend, Jaggers the lawyer and his savage female servant.

If one encounters Dickens at a young age, as I did, his minor characters seem bizarre, so strange that surely they could never exist in life. Years pass, life beyond the confines of books becomes clearer, and suddenly these odd creatures are everywhere: selling tickets in a theatre, waiting on tables, sitting at the next table in a restaurant, driving the bus.

The explanation is simple: Dickens paid attention and wrote about what he saw. He was not a fantasist, inventing odd creatures to keep the reader turning pages. This is life: people are strange. And from this comes the realization that to many people reading our own character, we can seem just as strange.

The minor characters became more recognizable as I read the book again and again over the years; so, too, did Pip and his striving to become a gentleman. Most people want to rise in the world, most people want to be admired by the people around them. Pip, poor boy, forgets to pay attention or pass judgement on who is around him and thus becomes a fop and not a gentleman. He can fence and is taught to hold his pinkie away from the handle of his cup when he takes tea, and so he thinks himself a gentleman.

It is only when he must act with compassion and love, and puts his life and future at risk to save a person who loves him, that Pip understands what it is to be a man. The scene is Dickens at his best, and he spares us no outrageous sentimental trick. It would make a stone weep.

Pip loses everything: position, wealth, future, all hope of great expectations. Only then, Dickens tells us, is Pip fully human and thus ready for, and deserving of, a life filled with great expectations.

The seemingly random characters are all connected in the end; nothing is forgotten or left to chance; there are scenes of terror and horror; there is comedy, and there is pain. No wonder, then, that for the sheer delight of his storytelling, Dickens is at the top of the list of great English novelists.

Regina

Earlier in my career as a writer, in 1995, I found myself with a prostitute as a central character in my fourth Brunetti novel, *Death and Judgment*, or perhaps it's better to say that I found myself in possession of a prostitute as a character but had no idea what she would do in the book or what would happen to her. As the book continued to develop, this character – rather like Topsy in *Uncle Tom's Cabin* – 'just growed.'

There she was, and her presence forced me to realize how very little I knew about prostitutes. I'd read about them, of course, in newspapers, magazines, novels (where they almost always had hearts of gold and died violently, often for love). They also did a lot of self-sacrificing (usually to help their male client/lover), and, rather in the fashion of another class of women I'd read about but not met, Indian wives, they seemed to spend their time in search of a funeral pyre upon which to immolate themselves to add to the happiness of other people.

In novels and films, they did not have blinking neon 'WHORE' signs on their front doors, nor did they all wear a whore uniform: short skirt, tight white sweater with low, scooped neckline, high heels, very visibly bleached hair, and – but only if they had rich clients – a poodle. In fact, they didn't have much of anything, certainly not personalities, although some of them could, when it proved necessary, make clever, sarcastic comments about their state. At least in films.

Because this occurred pre-Google, I had no choice but to do what writers and journalists had been doing for millennia: talk to people. A former student of mine was working as a counsellor for immigrant women who had been trafficked into Italy and forced into prostitution. The newspapers had been filled with this for ages, as they still are, decades later, and I quickly came to realize that there was little about their experiences with which I was not already familiar.

As a middle-class woman, I did feel a bit awkward telling my friend he was trying to introduce me to the wrong type of prostitute. I was looking for someone whose view of the profession was neutral – it was a job – and I wanted to know why they had chosen this job instead of, say, being a nurse or a history teacher or an accountant. I suppose my curiosity was capitalistic: I wanted to know their business model.

He mentioned a good friend, her name was Regina, whom he called a 'sex worker', fiercely engaged in the attempt to have her profession declared to be just that, a profession. At that time, sex workers could not pay taxes and thus would receive no pension when they retired.

Never able to miss making a joke, I raised my hands in the air and said, 'Every Italian's dream. And they complain?'

Looking confused, he said, 'I don't understand.'

'You said they can't pay taxes.'

He sighed, forgave me, and explained. Thus I was led, like an innocent lamb, into the legal world that has grown, failed, evolved, weakened, strengthened, and finally collapsed under the weight of all the contradictions during the Italian state's attempts to deal with both sex workers and their clients.

There appears to be no law against prostitution, which is defined as the exchange of sexual acts for money; at least, it's not a crime for the sex worker. To solicit a sexual act is illegal, but performing it in a house or apartment is 'tolerated', although illegal. In short, there is confusion about whether prostitution is exploitation or work.

Unwilling to say more because to discuss these laws paves the path to madness, he offered to call his friend, who was also the chairperson of an organization fighting for the normalization of the legal status of sex workers. No sooner had I said I'd like to meet Regina than he called her and arranged for me to have lunch at her home a few days later.

Please bear in mind that all of this took place almost thirty years ago; the laws concerning prostitution have changed since then, though nothing seems to have been made clearer. What has worsened the situation for women is the increase in the arrival of immigrant women who are brought into the country in the belief that they will be given legitimate work, but upon their arrival they are forced by various criminal gangs into prostitution and from then on are little more than slaves. No one knows how many women have entered Italy – legally and illegally – over the last few decades. But in total, there might be more than 100,000 prostitutes nowadays. Their clients per year are said to be three million.

I found Regina's home with little difficulty amidst endless fields and farms near Pordenone, a city about an hour north of Venice. The two-storeyed house was fenced off from fields of grapes and what appeared to be newly planted olive trees. The grass around the house had been recently cut and raked.

A woman about my age came from the house, followed by what appeared to be a mixed regiment of dogs.

Taller than I, blue eyes, upright posture, she smiled, shook hands, and invited me round to the back of the house, where a lunch was set and waiting on a circular table covered with a white linen tablecloth that reached the ground. The laden table was far different from what I had expected, though I don't remember what that was. I noticed that her dark hair was greying, although she wasn't yet fifty. She saw me studying the table. 'All from our garden,' she said, explaining that she shared the house with Clara, a colleague from work.

'Which I take care of,' said someone on the other side

of the old-fashioned curtain of long plastic strips hanging in the doorway that led from the house to the patio. A
short woman with blonde hair cut to her shoulders slowly
backed through the curtain, carrying a salad bowl the size
of a Galapagos turtle. She set it on the table and came over
to shake my hand. 'I'm Clara,' she said and welcomed me
to their house, speaking in the familiar '*tu*', as though we
were already friends.

And so it continued, friendly from the first, as we each
told a bit about ourselves: where we'd lived as children,
family, school, jobs, and how we'd ended up at this table.
They took turns going into the kitchen to come back with
pasta, vegetables, vegetables, vegetables, bread, as the
conversation turned to their profession. As I spooned up
more tomatoes, I felt something stroking against my left
thigh, the side closer to Clara.

Giving Clara the smile that used most of my teeth, I
shifted in my chair, crossed my legs the other way, and
turned my body towards Regina, who was busy shooing
away a goat that had wandered in from their field and
whose place at table I seemed to have stolen.

We all agreed that it was therapeutic to have animals, and I rattled out the standard clichés, my mind
busy with other thoughts. And then it came, the same
light pressure, but this time on my right thigh. They'd
each spoken of their long-time companions, in both
cases male police officers. So the police would be no
help, would they?

I decided that it was time to find out what was going on. I dropped my fork. In one quick motion, I grabbed a handful of tablecloth, as though I needed it to soak up water I'd spilled. As part of the same crafty gesture, I bent down and looked under the table to see what I could see.

And saw three dogs wandering around under there in festive joy to have a new person to be nice to. Seeing me, they came over and sat in a row, wagging their tails.

I dropped the tablecloth in front of them and went back to the conversation that had just begun: the story of Regina's experience with one of the serial killers of Udine.

In those years, the late 70s and early 80s, one serial killer murdered four women (it's always women, isn't it?) in the northern province of Udine, not far from where Regina and Clara lived. And worked. This one had been arrested. At the same time, another murdered fourteen women but was never found.

They explained that their work routine was this: they parked their cars by the side of the highway; a client drove up and bargained over the price; when that was agreed, the sex worker and the client retired further back into the undergrowth, either on foot or in the client's car, where they did whatever had been agreed upon, money changed hands, and the client drove off.

Because they were (dare I use this expression?) freelance, they had the liberty to decline an offer they found unsatisfactory or a person who made them uneasy. As they were self-employed, they also kept the money they earned.

Both of them spoke with understanding of and compassion for the foreign women who were forced to work for pimps or gangs: they could not refuse a client who demanded unprotected sex – this during the years when AIDS was killing its way through the world – nor could they deny any offer, no matter how miserable (in both the physical and the financial sense).

'If we had a union, they'd have some rights,' Regina said. She spoke from the position of someone with a companion who was a policeman and a mortgage that had been paid off. 'And the police would try to find this murderer,' she added, agitated by real anger. Rosa Luxemburg, you did not die in vain!

I think it was her anger that led her to tell me about her experience with what she believed was the serial killer.

Middle-aged, tall: that's all she remembered, save that his licence plate was from the province of Udine – this was a time when all Italian plates carried the initials of the province where the car was registered. She also remembered the first number that followed the initials.

One lazy summer afternoon, when Clara was with a client, he pulled up behind Regina's parked car and got out. Addressing her with the formal '*lei*', he asked how much she wanted and did not bargain over the price. He went back to his car and opened the door for her, then returned to the driver's seat. 'Put on your seatbelt, please,' he told her, and the uneasy feeling she'd had when he spoke to her diminished.

He took the car a hundred metres or so on the unpaved lane that went back into the bushes and then into the woods, switched off the motor, and turned towards her.

That's when she knew, she told me, and was careful to smile at him. He slid onto her seat and began to run his hands up and down her arms, then tightened them around her neck and began to strangle her.

Instead of screaming, Regina gave a passionate sigh and whispered, 'Oh, that's wonderful. Wonderful.' She moaned in anticipation of what was coming and tried to talk. He loosened his grip, and she told him he was wonderful, and he loosened his fingers and let her breathe. She praised him, said he was a real man, and what a shame to waste it in a car. Did he have a blanket? She wanted to be naked on it, on the grass with him.

She moved her hand and covered one of his, opened the door beside her and, when he released both his hands, began to open the front of her dress. But . . . it was a pity to be so uncomfortable. She wanted to feel the grass under them, like teenagers.

She slid down onto the grass, and he followed her. She kicked off her shoes, took off her dress and then her underwear. Naked now, she asked him to take the keys out of the ignition and get the blanket from the boot of his car. And hurry: she didn't know how long she could wait.

As he reached in to get the blanket, she got to her feet

and slammed the boot on his back, then took off running towards the main road. She heard shouting behind her but kept running. At the road, there was no sign of Clara. So she ran to the middle and waved her arms to try to stop cars. A few passed; people slowed, then drove away.

Finally, a man stopped and she got into the car, crying hysterically and telling the man that someone had tried to kill her and to drive away quickly. He did drive away, but not quickly, because he had his right hand over her breast.

Regina screamed and kicked the gearstick of the car, bringing it to a stop and, she hoped, doing at least some damage to the engine.

She stood by the road again, her hands pressed together, as if in prayer. Finally, a woman stopped and asked her where she could take her. 'The police, the police,' Regina tried to say.

At the police station, the woman went inside first and emerged from the building with a blanket and a police jacket, then Regina was helped inside.

When she had stopped crying – it was very difficult to imagine this quick-witted, strong-spirited woman cry – she told the police what had happened, where her car was parked, and tried to give the police the first number of the man's licence plate. Since she also remembered its Udine registration and what kind of car it was and its colour, she was offering the police more than enough information to lead them to the owner, but they seemed uninterested.

Regina

The fact that she was naked didn't help, nor did the fact that she was a sex worker known to the police. After another half hour or so, they let her go, asking her to return the blanket and the jacket when she could.

'So I don't have much hope they'll find the killer,' she said bitterly.

And they didn't.

Trips

San Gennaro

Some years ago, I found myself in Naples, a guest of the parents of a friend whose family has been living there for hundreds of years. His mother, Giulia, who for many years served as the city's Councillor of Art, offered to show me 'a few things' that perhaps not every tourist would be able to see.

I arrived on 19 September, an auspicious day, I was told, the beginning of the three-day-long celebration of the Feast of San Gennaro, patron saint and protector of the city. Giulia suggested that, to participate in it, she'd take me to the Cattedrale di Santa Maria Assunta, patron and protector of the city. It is difficult to move through the crowded streets of Napoli, but it is even more difficult for anyone who is with Giulia because of the number of people who stop her to say hello and exchange information or good wishes. Or gossip. On the way, Giulia, a small, slim woman who manages to walk the streets with eel-like grace, would also occasionally pause to name the church or building we were passing. Our first was the Church of Santa Maria Francesca delle Cinque Piaghe, patron saint and protector of the city, where women who want to conceive can sit for a moment in *'la sedia della fertilità'* to encourage exactly that. Next came the church of Santa Maria Maddalena de' Pazzi, also a patron saint and protector of the city.

As we approached the cathedral, Giulia explained the story of San Gennaro. He was martyred in 305 – decapitated – but two ampoules of his blood were collected soon after his death and preserved for more than 1,700 years, until the present day. His blood does not follow the laws of nature – to make no mention of those of probability – and, three times a year, it turns liquid in those tiny ampoules.

The cathedral was not at all crowded. Quite the opposite, for only a few people – perhaps twenty, surely no more – stood in line, facing an elaborately robed and mitred man whom Giulia told me was the Bishop of Naples.

We took our places at the end of the line, but since it was a Neapolitan line, it was oval and would probably have become circular had not the people in the middle refused to allow entry to those who tried to push themselves into it. As most of them had done.

We shuffled closer, Giulia serving as an icebreaker before me, familiar with the waters in which we found ourselves and attuned to any attempt to slip around or past us. I closed in behind her and whispered, 'What do we do?'

'Do what I do,' she answered, taking a small step

forward and blocking a tall, thin man who was attempting to encroach upon us from the left. Putting a hand on
her hip, she suddenly turned in my direction, driving her
elbow into the man's waist and leaving him bent over
while we advanced a few steps.

I moved to the left and suddenly had a clear line of
sight to the events taking place in front of me. The man
in the vestments held a large golden monstrance at
breast height. A small, dark object hung suspended in
the middle, supported by the two hands of the bishop
and by what appeared to be two golden angels, wings
folded and turned towards those of us waiting our turn.
At the sudden appearance of Giulia's head, the object
moved lower, she leaned forward, and then it suddenly
reappeared as she moved back from having kissed it.

Kissed the object? Kissed?

She stepped aside, and I thought for a moment of dis-
playing Christian charity and renouncing my place in line
to the wounded man we'd left behind. But then I heard
the voices of my Irish Catholic ancestors, those believers
in saints and fairies, in faith and magic, and I took a rather
large and courageous step forward and gave the air in
front of whatever it was the audible smack of a kiss, then
stepped quickly out of range.

Our duty done, Giulia and I moved to the left and sat
in the first chairs we found, mingling with a group of nine
or ten women: all old, all with long, grey hair straggling
down their backs, many toothless, and all singing.

But they were not really singing so much as chanting. I lowered my head and asked Giulia, 'What is it?'

'The descendants of San Gennaro,' she answered.

Descendants? A saint killed 1,700 years ago? Descendants of a priest?

But then the chant resumed, a wailing gasp, a high-pitched noise: I cannot call it a tune, nor yet a melody. It was an invocation, an expression of limitless pain at the death of San Gennaro. It was suddenly much cooler in the cathedral; Giulia felt it too, and pulled her scarf tighter around her neck.

If I had to record what they chanted, the best I could do is write '*zuuuu . . . diggadid . . . sssunns*', or any other human noise filled with the mystery of a faith that went back a few thousand years and dealt with death and blood and rebirth, though not necessarily that of Jesus Christ.

Giulia put her hand on my shoulder and we left, the voices of these women scurrying after us. It is the strangest sound I've ever heard: faintly threatening, faintly unworldly, but based on pain that must be made bearable. And blood.

Another vial of liquefying blood is kept at the Church of San Gregorio Armeno, patron saint and protector of the city, as well as of Armenia. It is that of Santa Patrizia, patron saint and protector of the city and of pilgrims, believed to be a descendant of the Emperor of Byzantium, a beautiful young woman who wanted no pomp or wealth and desired only to live a life of prayer as a nun. She was – as are many of the heroines in fairy tales – beautiful, noble, virtuous, and uninterested in marriage, and, like many good heroines, gave all she owned to the poor. She attempted to flee a forced marriage by sailing from Constantinople, but died – apparently having chosen the wrong map – in a shipwreck off the coast of Naples.

Her relics are kept in the Church of San Gregorio Armeno, among them the ampoule with her blood. This blood is said to liquefy each year on 25 August, although – no doubt because it is the blood of a woman – it has been reported to liquefy on other, unpredictable dates and seems to lack the professional rigour of San Gennaro. The Church of San Gregorio Armeno and its convent are a large complex of buildings that could easily remain unnoted by a person walking past. When I visited, the street leading to the entrance was deserted and discreet; at the end of it, Giulia's son, Giulio, stood in front of the closed gate, waiting for us. We arrived only minutes before the door was pulled open by an elderly nun wearing the white and black habit of the Crucified Sisters Adorers of the Eucharist. Her hands, hidden under her scapular, released themselves when she saw Giulia, and there was an exchange of affection and regard. Giulio stood respectfully aside and came along with us when the nun turned to take us to the Mother Superior.

Following the old nun, we moved slowly and thus had time to see gold, light, portraits, thick silver candelabra, golden monstrances on gilded altars. We walked past glory, stepped on glistening tiles; we peered through doorways and saw portraits of saints and angels, Christ and his mother, an abattoir of martyrdom.

We passed through an enclosed garden filled with avocado trees, then another with clementines. We quickly lost all sense of where we were, although every so often we heard the beep of horns from the city. Without that assurance, we could easily have thought ourselves transported into the past. Suddenly the nun slowed her pace and stopped in front of a large wooden door. Turning to us, she said, 'This is the convent.'

And so it proved to be. A younger woman dressed in the same habit of the Crucified Sisters Adorers of the Eucharist opened the door, smiled, and welcomed us. The older nun addressed her as *'Madre'* and told her that we were the friends of the bishop who had come to see the relics. I glanced aside at Giulia, who seemed the most likely of the three of us to be a 'friend of the bishop', but she was busy examining her shoes.

The nun who had been our guide nodded to us and took her leave. The Mother Superior suggested we begin, addressing me as *'Dottoressa'*, a title I quite enjoyed the sound of. I returned the courtesy, referring to her as *'Madre'*, though she could easily have been my daughter, perhaps even my granddaughter.

With no further delay, she pulled an enormous ring of keys from the pocket of her habit and ran them familiarly through her hands until she found the one she wanted. She led us along the corridor, then stopped and opened a door on the left.

Slipping her hand inside, she felt for the switch on the wall, and something approaching the intensity of daylight filled the windowless room. When I opened my eyes, I saw gold everywhere, especially in the halos hovering above the heads of the saints in the paintings. Legend claims that Saint Peter told the wicked Romans he was unworthy of being crucified upright, like his master, and asked them, please, could they crucify him upside down? Either they denied the requests of all Christians or the painter had refused, for this Peter, recognizable by the keys of the kingdom of heaven he carried, stood on his feet. I saw small portraits of Santa Lucia, her eyes carefully placed on a plate beside her; Saint Agatha gazing sadly at her breasts, placed on a somewhat larger dish; St Lawrence on his grill, Santa Caterina d'Alessandria with her spiked wheel; and a few I didn't recognize, as sometimes happens when there are too many people at a party and it's impossible to keep them all straight.

After showing us the statues and portraits, the Mother Superior moved on to the relics, of which there seemed to be an inordinate number. As she was explaining whose toe it was in that box, which saint had owned the bloody cloth in the glass case, my memory turned to – of all things – *The Canterbury Tales* and to the one damned soul amidst all those lusty and unreliable scamps and cheaters, adulterers and liars.

The Pardoner, a man who made a living by selling indulgences and relics, has had a drink too many and reveals his method for procuring the relics he sells to those gullible enough to buy. He's got a bag full of pig bones he's picked up in a garbage heap and offers to sell them to the other pilgrims, along with the pillowcase he's selling as Mary's veil.

When my attention returned, I heard the Madre Superiore saying that the nails from Christ's cross were the supreme treasures of their collection.

One of us asked how many there were: 'Three?' That's the usual number if a monastery or a church has managed to get them all: one for each hand and a longer one for the feet.

After a moment's hesitation, she said, 'Four,' and I found it best to return my thoughts to Chaucer.

Master and Commander

First things first: let's dismiss any idea of impartiality or measured, neutral judgement in this review. Toss out of the window even-handedness, restraint, objectivity. I do not like Patrick O'Brian: I adore him. From the beginning of my addiction, I waited with slack-jawed impatience for the arrival of each new book. When I finished number nineteen, *The Hundred Days*, I read with a battering heart the news that O'Brian planned to bring his three-decade-old series of sea novels to an end with the next book. The prospect had me desolate, no consolation possible but to hurl myself into rereading the novels, and where better to start than with *The Mauritius Command*, the fourth book in the series?

The basic conceit that propels the books is a common one, with distant ancestors in the Achilles–Patroclus friendship and closer relatives in the to-death bond between Butch Cassidy and the Sundance Kid: guys are pals and they have adventures. Just as the Greeks had the Trojans, and Butch and the Kid had the Bolivians, O'Brian's heroes have Napoleon and the French. (After reading all of the books, it is impossible to write that last noun without instinctively adding the adjective 'wicked'.)

In this case, the guys are Jack Aubrey, an officer in the King's Navy, and Stephen Maturin, a ship's surgeon who is also, and just as importantly, a spy. The adventures start when they first join ship in *Master and Commander* and begin to sail the known world, on Jack's part in search of enemy ships to capture or destroy; on Stephen's, to overturn the plots and ploys of the wicked French.

And what ships they sail! Like Athens, nineteenth-century England's best defence was her wooden walls, those masterpieces of human creation that manage to circumnavigate the globe, as the characters never tire of saying, 'as easy as kiss your hand', and to withstand storms that batter them with waves twice and thrice their height, yet which often provide sailing easy enough to allow Jack on his violin and Stephen on his cello endless hours to play the Locatelli and Handel sonatas and duets they love so well.

And here lies part of the secret that has led people as sophisticated as A. S. Byatt and Iris Murdoch to enlist under Jack's flag: these are not cardboard cut-out figures in the manner of Captain Horatio Hornblower or the Scarlet Pimpernel, characters with all the emotional and intellectual depth of Mickey Mouse. Instead, they are fully realized, at times painfully complex men whose tangled humanity jumps up from the pages and strikes the reader with a living sense of just how like us they are.

Take away the lace-trimmed uniforms, peel off the elaborate wigs, and they are men who agonize over the need to send other men off to their deaths and who weep when those men die; they are husbands who long passionately for their wives while knowing they will never fully understand those women; and they are men who argue about slavery, capital punishment, the position of women, and, yes, about good and evil. In a reflection upon the difference between the conquered and the conqueror, Stephen offers this: 'A conquering race, in the place of that conquest, is rarely amiable; the conquerors pay less obviously than the conquered, but perhaps in time they pay even more heavily, in the loss of the humane qualities.'

During the course of the series, the two men mature and increase in complexity. Jack first appears as a brash youth whose reluctance to submit to the iron discipline of the navy leads him to endure harsh punishment; age and increased rank make him understand the absolute necessity of that discipline and impel him, however reluctantly, to impose it upon his own men. Stephen brings with him a painful history: born of mixed Irish and Spanish blood, he must opt to support his country's historical persecutor, England, because he sees it as the lesser evil compared to the megalomaniacal ambitions of Napoleon. Jack's response to life is almost always impulsive: he is led by his heart and, as Stephen often laments, by his prick. In Stephen, O'Brian has found the perfect foil for Jack: the saturnine doctor's heart too often lies dormant, leaving only his broad-reaching intellect to lead him through life. As the books never cease to prove, both paths are equally flawed, and it is only in the combination of both, mirrored in the ever-maturing friendship and love between them, that the golden mean of a sane life becomes possible.

The virtues of the series are amply evident in *The Mauritius Command*. At the opening, Jack Aubrey is landbound, having lost his commission and been put on half pay. Life on land for Jack always proves a disaster: his beehives have been destroyed by wax moths; the cow is barren and refuses the attentions of the bull; his garden is a collection of grotesque, stunted plants. The personal realm is not much different: his mother-in-law has invaded his home, his wife is observed by Stephen to have the 'frigid' English look, and his only progeny are a pair of bald and dribbling twins, both, alas, girls.

As often happens, he is saved by Stephen, who brings him the news that the wicked French have sent four new frigates to their base on the island of Mauritius, from where they plan to snatch up the richly laden Indiamen sailing home for England, thus striking a severe blow to the British economy. Jack cannot believe the British Naval Ministry could treat this as a serious danger until Stephen cynically points out that many members of the Admiralty Board are also stock owners of the East India Company, and thus 'there is likely to be a wonderful degree of celerity in this case'.

So it quickly proves, and with the resulting speed they

are given the command to set sail aboard the *Boadicea*. Although the navy has more than a thousand ships, Stephen has but to name her for Jack to identify her instantly as 'Thirty-eight. A weatherly ship, though slow.' Furthermore, we learn, her sailing would be immeasurably improved by more careful stowing of her hold and by the use of cross-cat-harpins and Bentinck shrouds. And here lies another marvel of these books. All of them are filled with references to naval arcana that can have clear meaning only to those who have spent decades at sea. There is frequent talk of close-rigged topsails, the driver-boom, the orlop: heaven (or sailors) alone knows what they are, just as it alone understands the imperative necessity of having the weather gauge or going about on the starboard tack.

Regardless of the depth of our ignorance about these things, the urgency of accomplishing or avoiding them is made real and present on every page. So, too, is the delight we come to take in seaboard dinners that offer us spotted dick, 'drowned baby', or 'soused hog's face'. And after we've stowed aboard with Stephen for a while, we come to share his delight and wonder at a fleeting glimpse of a manatee or a crested mousebird.

But, like O'Brian, I have digressed, leaving our heroes on the year-long voyage toward the Mauritius Islands. Promoted to commodore, Jack sails in command of three other captains, and their portraits show O'Brian at his psychological best. One is a steady, dull seaman; the second is a flogging brute, feared and hated by his entire crew; while the third is a nobleman, a prancing popinjay whose cabin looks as though 'a brothel had moved into a monastery', yet who has somehow managed to win the loyalty of his men. It is to prove a disastrous combination for the squadron, as each of these men, driven by his private demons, leads his ship and crew to disaster.

Driven by the ever-present sense of urgency that ruled these ships, the squadron sails to its first victory and then into the eye of a hurricane. Another blazingly described battle quickly follows, and O'Brian shows how a trifle as insignificant as a carelessly discarded flag can flip the shuttlecock of victory to the other side. Chaucer writes that Fortune goes 'now up, now down, like bucket in a well,' and so it proves here: superior numbers are meaningless, greater firepower is to no avail, for whorish victory often follows the less worthy man.

Though Jack is known in the fleet as 'Lucky Jack Aubrey', the profits and joys of his victories against the wicked French are often snatched from him by jealous rivals in the British Navy and by the mechanism of its all-devouring bureaucracy. So too, it would seem, at the end of *The Mauritius Command*, when a fresh squadron brings news that shatters Jack's professional hopes. But Fortune smiles, and the same long-delayed mailbag carries a letter from home bringing him news that raises him to a peak of joy and optimism.

This, perhaps, is the prevailing sense of the books, a benevolent optimism that can look on savagery and bloody slaughter and still find comfort in the daily grind of ordinary life and in the heartfelt faith of these two fine men: with effort and by holding true to principle, the good shall prevail. It is a sign of O'Brian's genius that the reader has no choice but to believe it.

The Beauty of the Unknown

I confess that when I first heard the subject I was asked to write about – the Beauty of the Unknown – I was more than a little perplexed, for my trite and literal mind leaped to the realization that what is unknown is unlikely to be anywhere at all on the scale from ugliness to beauty by reason of definition: that which is unknown is also unseen, unheard, unscented, and untouched. Am I leaving something out here? Yes, untasted. Thus it is as difficult for it to be beautiful as it is for it to be ugly. Because it's unknown, right?

This led me to figure that these sly devils at the Innsbruck Festival of Early Music had something up their sleeves: an idea, probably, perhaps even a clever one, for all I knew, even something that was intended to lead people to think about beauty.

And then I stopped fooling around and began to think about it. It seems to me that – given the impossibility of the phrase – the beauty some of us invest in the idea of the unknown must result from the desire to find it, and that desire comes from the imagination, which creates an idea of the unknown. Think for a moment of those nineteenth-century British explorers who went off in search of unknown continents, unknown cultures, unknown conquests. Stanley wanted to cross Africa, but had no idea how to do it, or, for that matter, where to go. Livingstone wanted to convert the unknown heathen and find the unknown source of the Nile and in the doing found 'scenes so lovely they must have been gazed on by angels in their flight'. Mungo Park, searching for Timbuktu, naked, lost, 500 miles from the nearest European settlement, wrote that 'the extraordinary beauty of a small moss irresistibly caught my eye.' All found the unknown to be beautiful.

It was not only the British who responded to the beauty of the unknown: Ibn Battuta, the fourteenth-century Moroccan traveller, often remarked upon the beautiful things he observed while travelling more than 75,000 miles over the course of decades.

But before we go all starry-eyed about the beauty of the unknown, let us consider the words of Mr Kurtz, whose attempt to bring enlightenment to darkest Africa Joseph Conrad considered in *Heart of Darkness*. Intoxicated by the unknown, Kurtz went to Central Africa in search of it. And found it. When the narrator asks Kurtz what he has found, here in the Unknown, safe within his compound, under the windows of which are exposed the desiccated heads of the people he has killed, Kurtz reveals to him the nature of the Unknown. 'The horror. The horror.'

These men, the cultural ancestors of the twenty to

thirty million tourists who flood into Venice each year, searched for the geographical unknown, though photography and television force a redefinition of what unknown means. Others, like Howard Carter, the discoverer of the tomb of King Tutankhamun, searched for the unknown past. When Carter trained a flashlight into the room where Tut's remains had slept away thousands of years, he was asked if he saw anything. 'Yes,' he answered. 'Wonderful things.'

I think that's what the search for the unknown is all about: wonderful things, beautiful things. The imagination tells us, most often, that the Unknown is beautiful or desirable (think of veiled women, gift-wrapped packages, a provocative sexual suggestion). This belief is animated by something profound in us all: the desire to know, learn, discover, and experience pleasure. Part of the pleasure or the beauty, I believe, lies in the pursuit of the unknown, the perpetual renewal of imaginative pleasure as we grow closer to that Unknown.

'Heard melodies are sweet, but those unheard are sweeter.' Again, my thoughts turn to an English poet, Keats, who said this two hundred years ago. Unheard melodies are sweeter. How often the imagination serves as a trampoline, hurling us ever higher in spirit at the thought of what is to come rather than at the sound of what is or has been.

It is one of the essential glories of opera that each performance takes us to the unknown. Yes, we know the libretto and we know the music, and perhaps we have heard the same singers, or some of them, before; perhaps we have even seen earlier performances with this same cast. But that night, that performance, those minutes as the music is played for us, are unknown. Familiar, perhaps, but unknown.

Many people, I assume, have attended numerous performances of a run of the same opera, and thus know how different the experience of seeing each separate performance is from punching the 'replay' button on a CD player. No aria is sung the same way, the dramatic tension is not the same: some nights it's flabby and dull, and other nights the drama grabs you by the throat and shakes you till you see double. Some nights you yearn for real bullets in the rifles used to shoot the tenor who is singing Cavaradossi, while other nights in the same run you gasp in horror as Cavaradossi falls and the unknowing Tosca cries out '*Ecco un artista.*'

If this were not the case, then there would be no sense in leaving the house to go to a live performance. We could all stay home and listen to CDs and watch opera videos.

But we don't, and I think the reason lies in the beauty of the unknown. Why else the success of the Met simulcast? Each performance will be different, in larger or smaller ways, and the fact of their being different is exciting, sometimes thrilling. No staging is the same: Rigoletto is a monster or a doting father worthy of pity; Fiordiligi and Dorabella do or don't realize who the fake Albanians are; *Giulio Cesare* is serious drama or ironic comment on human weakness. And those, like me, who are opera junkies know that no aria is ever the same, not really.

People often say that books change when we read them in greater age. But they don't. It is we who change. With a book, there is no performance, nothing new, nothing different, at least not in the text.

But music is ever new, and each performance is, for us, the first time we've ever heard the piece. Thus we sit there, watching and listening, perhaps to an opera we have seen dozens of times, and yet, and yet, we are there to discover the beauty of the Unknown.

Behind the Scene

A New Case for Brunetti

It is hardly my place to speak of how writers in general approach their work: I know few writers, and those I do know tend to speak of things other than work. But it seems to me that writers, in general, either do or do not know what is going to happen. In a way, one might say that they either have or have not taken a peek at the last page before they begin to write the first.

Some writers make a complete outline, write long biographies of all of the characters who will appear in the story, understand all of the relationships among events and among characters, all of this before they begin writing. Then there are the rest of us who turn on the computer and begin.

In my own case, I usually need either an opening scene or a reason why all the things that are going to happen in the book – whatever those things turn out to be – are going to happen. That is, I need an opening scene that will grab the reader's attention, or I need a motive that will explain sufficiently why the characters in the book are motivated to do what they do.

To speak specifically with reference to my own books, I can give the example of *Blood from a Stone*, which deals with the African vendors, *vu cumprà*, who sell counterfeit designer bags on the streets of Venice. The idea for this book came to me years ago as I was walking through Campo Santo Stefano a few days before Christmas. As I walked between the wooden stalls where food and tourist junk was being sold, I saw, stretching out on both sides of the pavement that led from the *campo* to the Accademia Bridge, two rows of Black street sellers, standing over their exposed wares.

I quite literally stopped in my tracks, stared at them, and found myself saying, out loud, 'My God, there's a book.' I had, for more than a decade, been seeing them, walking past them, even talking about them with my friends. But I had never stopped and *looked* at them, which means I'd never considered who they might be, why they might be there, what their private lives might be like. And so I knew, in that instant, that the next book would deal with the *vu cumprà*.

Because, at that time, I knew nothing about them, I had no idea what the book would do with them or how they would behave in the book or what they would be involved with, other than selling their bags. As I watched, the opening scene played itself across my imagination: two men slip through the crowds of shoppers and tourists, suddenly appear in front of one of the *vu cumprà*, and shoot and kill him before slipping through the astonished bystanders to disappear into the streets leading from the *campo*. It was only later, after I'd spent months working on that opening scene and its consequences, that I began to see why he might have been murdered.

Crime needs a motive. Ten years before, I had read newspaper accounts of snuff films that were then being made in Bosnia. A snuff film is a kind of pornographic horror film in which a woman is repeatedly raped, then killed in a bloody fashion. Only it's real: she's really raped and killed. And people pay to buy them and look at them.

I found the idea so appalling that I knew that the next book, no matter what would happen during the course of it, would be propelled by those films, and that the production and distribution of those films would be the motive for whatever murders eventually took place.

When I started the book, I was helped by another scene that appeared to me, that of a truck running off an ice-slicked road and bursting open to scatter bodies in the snow. Blood. White. Wheels spinning silently. Silence. Nice, huh?

Both as a reader and as a writer, I am of the opinion that readers are far more interested in discovering why things happened than they are in discovering the name of the person who did those things. It seems the most natural of questions to ask when we learn of something, whether it is the divorce of the people next door or the murder of a Mafia capo: Why? Why that person? And for what reason?

The opening line of Ruth Rendell's *A Judgement in Stone* names: the killer, the victims, and the motive. But that simple declarative sentence doesn't fully explain *why*. The book does, and with such brilliance that it remains, for me, one of the best crime novels.

On the Move

People move. Characters move. Life is filled with motion, and novels are filled with descriptions of that motion. Sounds simple enough, doesn't it? In real life, as we sit in a streetside café and watch people walk past, we see them move, overhear a snatch of conversation, watch them stop to emphasize a remark. Then off they go and we forget about them and return to our coffee.

But characters in a novel, that's a different thing. They walk by as the narrator sits at that same table, and it becomes the writer's job to make that event register with the reader. In a crime novel, the writer must move the villain to the place where he will commit his crime, and the good guy has to be moved around until he discovers who the villain is. But most of the motion that is described in a crime novel, indeed, in any novel, is relatively inconsequential. Characters go to sleep, get up, go to work, eat dinner, drink coffee, talk to friends, go back home. Readers follow along, and just as we lose patience with a tedious narrator, we grow bored if a writer describes purposeless events.

We are interested in the movements described in a

novel to the degree that the writer makes them meaning-
ful. Thus every event advances, however minimally, the
reader's understanding of plot and character.

I am not suggesting that every untied shoelace must
cause a fall and every letter contain a death threat or a
confession. Perhaps an example would help. A woman
trips and is helped to her feet. In real life, the scene might
stop there, with the woman safely on her feet and walking away after saying thank you.

In a novel, however, the scene opens up endless pos-
sibilities both for plot advancement and for character
revelation. A man helps her to her feet and offers her a
coffee: three months later, they're married. Six months
later, she's dead and he inherits the lot. Or the narrator
grudgingly helps her up, thinking that if she had had the
sense to wear flat shoes, she would not have fallen and
caused him to worry that he's hurt his back by bending
down. Or he watches another man come to her rescue and
feels anger – or envy – as the man runs his hand across her
hip and thigh as he helps her stand. Or the woman either
resents or enjoys the man's treatment.

The writer here is behaving like the Romanian trickster
on the bridge who waves his hands over the three walnut
shells on the portable table, under one of which there is a
pebble. Keep your eye on *this*, while I am busy with *that*.
Even if the woman disappears from the book, the business
of the book has been advanced because the reader now has
another piece of information, whether about the woman,

the man who helped her to her feet, or the man who saw him do it. Or all of them.

This incremental information moves the plot forward because it advances the reader's understanding of why or how a character acts. Just as easily, however, the reader is being prepared to respond with surprise when the character does something not at all in accord with what he has previously been revealed to be: the Romanian lifts the walnut shell, and the pebble's there.

Speech, too, creates motion, for the revelation of character that it causes will both enrich the reader's understanding and advance the motion of the plot. In life as in fiction, it is the most common form of revelation. I once heard a man explain how, after his wife had been in labour for seventeen hours with their first child, he was 'tired of listening to her complain'. (Because my mother taught me the rudiments of polite behaviour, I resisted the impulse to express the hope that his wife would have less trouble finding a good divorce lawyer.) Or think of someone who remarks that another person got what they deserved. His neighbour's gay son got AIDS? Mother Teresa got the Nobel Peace Prize? Oh my, what different souls these remarks reveal.

In real life, most conversation doesn't lead anywhere; most of it has the shelf life of overripe figs. But in a novel, the writer has an obligation to select those conversations that contain some nugget of information or revelation.

One example of the force a single remark can convey

occurs in Henry James's *The Portrait of a Lady*. Madame Merle, a woman with a past, has helped manipulate the heroine, Isabel Archer, into a marriage with a man so dreadful that he will destroy her every hope of happiness. Late in the novel, she reluctantly accepts the fact that she will not profit from Isabel's destruction and exclaims, 'Have I been so vile all for nothing?' One of the admirable qualities of the novels of Henry James is his characters' habit of always remaining fully clothed, but Madame Merle, had she removed all of her clothing, could not have revealed herself as fully as she does with this one remark.

The spoiled, sometimes aristocratic and often wealthy women of Jane Austen's novels compete with one another to reveal their arid hearts. My reader's heart, however, has always been in thrall to *Pride and Prejudice*'s Lady Catherine de Bourgh. She has but to open her mouth to reveal her head-spinning arrogance.

The great novels are filled with examples of physical motion used to express more than the process of getting from here to there. Austen's Lizzy Bennet rushes on foot to her sister's bedside, careless of how she arrives so long as it is by the quickest route. Rash and impetuous, she has no hesitation at 'jumping over stiles and springing over puddles with impatient activity', after which she arrives at the home of the Bingleys 'with weary ankles, dirty stockings, and a face glowing with the warmth of exercise.' Austen then uses her disordered state as a mirror in which to reflect the other characters. The women are shocked by such behaviour, one of the men can think only of his breakfast, but Mr Darcy is struck by 'the brilliancy which exercise had given to her complexion'.

Or think of Vronsky's fall from his racehorse, when Anna Karenina's failure to suppress her terror at his danger makes public their love to the people around her. Examples come crowding in, don't they? Emma Bovary's night-time carriage ride through the streets of Rouen, Marlow's trip upriver into the *Heart of Darkness*, Captain Ahab's pursuit of the White Whale. In pursuit of their own white whales, writers cast their characters into motion, drawing us, the readers, in their wake.

In the end, if the novel is to succeed, the reader must be moved to care deeply about the fate of these characters. They need not be good or virtuous people: Captain Ahab, Becky Sharp, and Patricia Highsmith's Ripley are strangers to virtue. Nor must they triumph, just as those three characters do not triumph. But they must be so completely and convincingly drawn that they move in the reader's mind from being characters in a book to people who are as vibrant as people in real life. Emily Dickinson wrote, 'Love is like Life – merely longer.' In the hands of great authors, characters are like real people, merely realer.

With a Little Help from Lew Archer

People sometimes ask me where the ideas for my books come from, and I try to explain that there's no way to know when they will come, nor from where. The only sure thing is that I know them when they arrive.

I have been rereading the crime novels of Ross Macdonald, a master of the genre who wrote a series of books featuring his detective, Lew Archer. Inevitably, when Archer is asked to investigate a case, he discovers that the problem he is examining today has its roots in events that took place fifteen or twenty years ago. One generation inherits crime or guilt or violence from the previous one, and only by trailing events back to their origins does Archer come to understand what is going on and how the past has come back to haunt the living.

During the time I was rereading Macdonald, I began a new Brunetti novel in which Brunetti was asked by a friend of the family to take a look at an accident that took place fifteen years before, in which a person was killed. The book began with the conversation in which the request was made, after which Brunetti started to examine the information from the past, and he indeed discovered that what looked at the time like an accident might well have been something more sinister.

The dead person was only a teenager at the time of death, and the sudden death cut off possibility just as it cut off life. I invented a witness to the accident who said that it wasn't an accident at all, but an attack.

After writing a hundred pages of the manuscript, I realized that the reader's sympathies were being elicited, time after time, for a character they'd never encountered and who had been dead for a decade and a half. Only the immediate family had known the victim as a living person, and that, I began to realize, put the reader's sympathy at a distance.

It's one thing to know a person and then have the person die: this creates the possibility for loss and grief, even the desire for revenge. But if the death took place fifteen years ago, there is no immediacy, and thus there is less passion, less pain, and, on the part of the reader, significantly less sympathy for the dead person. Consequently, there is less passion to discover who was responsible for the death.

What, then, I asked myself, if there had been no death, but only damage? What if the person had survived the same accident/attack and Brunetti had discovered that the damage was the result of an attempt to cause death?

If the character is resurrected but returned to life in a damaged state, the reader would see and hear the grim consequences of the injury each time the character appears or is discussed. Here is a person whose life was not lost or taken but someone whose life – rich at the time of the incident with endless promise and possibility – has been damaged irretrievably, who is condemned to live the rest of their life as a shadow of their former self.

So make the person sweet-tempered, throw in beauty and instinctive kindness, and here is a character who is not only sympathetic but also terribly wounded. The reader, led to like the character, can now sympathize with the victim of the tragic events and can feel the inexpressible loss of youth and promise and beauty. As a result, the reader now wants the person responsible for the crime to be found and punished because the consequences of the attack are evident, as are the grief and agony of the family of this shattered being.

The book remained faithful to the Ross Macdonald pattern: events from the past worm their way into and destroy the lives of people living in the present. It is only by understanding past events that the present can make sense.

More importantly, by keeping the character alive, the book moves from presenting a tragedy that is fifteen years old – long enough for most people to have forgotten it – and puts on the page a living person who will win the reader's sympathy and thus create pathos.

Amorality

Dirt

As my friends and I became more familiar with the military-controlled system of which we were such a teeny part, we were similarly learning about the characters of our colleagues. The bar at the Iran Tour Hotel, where all newly arrived employees were housed until they found acceptable accommodation, was famous for both its beer and its pistachios, a large dish of which accompanied every order, regardless of its size. The main room with the long bar and the frequently wiped tables was the favourite meeting place of the staff of our company, Telemedia (aka: Tell 'Em Anything). The people working for Bell Helicopter – our financial mother ship as well as the breast from which all of us nursed – were often former members of the US military. They scorned the bar at the Iran Tour and had little regard for the likes of us.

We were – oh, how does one best say this? – a variegated group of people, a mix of this and that, an odd lot. Soon after I arrived, I realized that most of the Telemedia staff referred to one another only by their initials, while employees of Bell Helicopter were addressed by their full or first name but never by their initials. Although I did not know the reason for this division, I was still much gratified the first time someone referred to me as 'DL'.

Let me pause here for a moment to discuss a question of deportment. It was clear from the beginning that no one much minded how we chose to conduct our emotional or erotic lives: they might have been open for conversation, but they were above criticism.

The only vice – if it is a vice – was venality. We were, all of us, earning wildly more than we had ever earned before and certainly more than we were worth, considering the amount of loafing, sleeping, flirting, lateness, absence, chatting, and general laziness that characterized the quality of our performance during most of our workdays. Pay day came once a month, when the representative of Bell Helicopter passed through our offices, handing out our pay cheques. I was not the first to whisper, 'Never have so many been paid so much for so little.'

Hence, any display of cheapness was noted. And punished. Their initials were taken from them, and in return they were given back their full name. For example, DW went to lunch with colleagues one fateful day and contested the bill, explaining that he had had a green salad, not the more expensive shrimp cocktail chosen by the others, and asked that the difference in price be part of the calculation of the bill. 'Sure thing, David Watson,' someone told him while handing him the change he'd requested. And FP boasted, the day before she returned to being called Frances Panna, that she had found a house for some newly arrived colleagues and had charged them a month's rent as her 'finder's fee'. No one spoke to either of them for a month.

Because we were meant to work as teachers, it was assumed that we all had at least a BA degree. To be eligible for promotion, higher degrees were required, a master's or a doctorate. Many people had them; some of them were real.

Bear in mind, please, that we were working for a civilian company, not for the US government. Thus, the more impressive our CV, the higher the salary our employer could charge the government for our services. And it was our company that authenticated the claims we made on our employment applications. Thus we were a smouldering heap of lies and exaggerations, some of us unable to tell a pronoun from a walrus, a verb from a pineapple.

It took some weeks before I learned the origin myth of the use of initials. The morning shift began at eight, the afternoon at four. At first, no doubt in concession to jet lag and the need to adjust to the new job, I had been assigned to the afternoon shift, but after a month or so, I was reassigned to the morning shift. The little yellow school bus dropped us at the school at 7.30. This meant we had a half hour in the teachers' break room, and it was to fill this time that 'Dirt' had been invented.

There were more or less equal numbers of men and women on the teaching staff. Some were away from home for the first time in their lives; many had never been in a foreign country. There were no parents, no spouses, no neighbours. No one to make a judgement. Like Adam and Eve, we lived in a virgin world. Some of the faculty, however, were indiscreet and would reveal, even boast of, their triumphs; others delighted in reporting the sexual conquests of others, even augmenting them. What better way to fill that half hour than by divulging names?

Let me pause here to introduce our superior, Colonel Peachy. He'd left the military years before, but he still wanted to be called 'Colonel', so 'Colonel' he was. It took him some weeks to learn of our pastime, but less than a day to have a notice posted on the wall of the teachers' room forbidding 'Dirt' and its 'shocking, distasteful revealing of the names and private lives of other employees of Bell Helicopter'. Ah, so that's what it was all about. Thus, just as the thumbs of animals that begin to climb trees will gradually evolve to face the other digits, creating a firm grip, a genetically modified version of 'Dirt' evolved.

By the next morning, the names of the staff had been erased, replaced by their initials. Thus 'VF' had gone for a 'WE' (weekend) in 'C' (Cairo) with 'AM', who, alas, was married to 'JP'.

Perhaps realizing that the voice of truth was not to be quelled, the Colonel never again tried to stuff the mouths of the serfs, and we continued with the early-morning revelations, even when 'DP' (who was British) had to go back to 'L' for a 'WE', where she would have an 'A'. The initials of the father were not given, although I've always suspected it was CB.

A few months later, Colonel Peachy, perhaps longing for revenge or those golden days when he was surrounded by soldiers, decided that members of the teaching staff would be obliged to wear the Telemedia uniform: white shirt, dark blue jacket (with a tie for men), and dark blue trousers (skirt optional for women). We received not only the notification of this new rule but also the form with which we could order our version of the uniform.

BB, who was an agitator, bless her, reminded us all that nothing obliged us to register the correct size for each piece of clothing. The people standing around her sighed deeply in admiration before filling out their forms.

Two months later, the packages were delivered to us during our tea break so that we had to open them in the presence of the Colonel. Much to my astonishment, I had been sent a size 4 jacket and size 48 trousers. As for the white shirts, one was extra small and the other extra large. Strangely enough, similar mistakes had been made in the delivery of the uniforms for all the women employees, and the only thing to do was to return the uniforms to the company that had sent them.

The Colonel was said to have been apoplectic and called a general meeting for the following afternoon, cancelling all classes, the first and only time this happened during my four years of working for him.

By 5 p.m., we were all gathered in a tent the military

used for meetings: there must have been forty of us. Colonel Peachy arrived at five after, and walked down the aisle that divided the tent into two sides.

He took some notecards from his pocket, set them on the podium in front of him and paused, not bothering to look at his audience. Had he done so, he might have noticed that many of the male teachers were wearing skirts. Or that most of the women were wearing ties, even those most generously endowed, all of whom had held their breath while dressing and managed to shove their bosoms into extra-small shirts. We looked, perhaps, like circus clowns, but we felt like tigers.

The Colonel's dramatic pause before beginning his speech extended a few seconds too many, for as he opened his mouth to start, the back flap of the tent was pulled slowly open and BB appeared in her new Telemedia uniform. Red shoes with six-inch heels. Fine black stockings with a heavy black line going up the back. Teeny, size 4 uniform skirt, the hem of which flirted with her knees from above. White shirt, size extra small, open to the fourth button so as better to expose both her bosom and her brassiere, which was red. Two–foot-long cigarette holder, cigarette already lit. RED lipstick and an insubordinate amount of mascara. Black top hat.

Saying nothing, she walked down the aisle towards the Colonel, who appeared to have suffered some sort of paralyzing enemy nerve-gas attack.

BB walked towards him, her hips moving in an inter-rogatory manner. She stopped at the second row and slipped into a seat on the aisle that happened to be free.

From the back, one of the Colonel's officers asked, 'Anything else, Colonel?'

'No.'

Janus-Faced Deity

One of the most delightful rewards of having become a published writer of crime fiction is to have made the acquaintanceship, and then the friendship, of Baroness Ruth Rendell, a writer for whom I have the highest respect, and the crime writer whose talent I most envy. I was a fan long before I became a friend, and that last came about because Ruth was a judge on the Booker Prize jury with a friend of mine who, when I sat at dinner singing her praises, asked if I'd like to meet her. The only greater joy he might have offered me would be the chance to sing Handel's *Alcina* at Covent Garden. The prospect of meeting her seemed only minimally less frightening, for I was not at all sure I'd be up to the task.

It was quickly arranged for the next time I was in London. After meeting at a restaurant, we were polite in that stiff, British way while both of us, I suppose, wondered what we were going to talk about. As it turned out, we started to talk about books, and continued to do so for years. It is quickly said: Ruth had read everything. Well, most of my friends have read everything because most of us have spent the bulk of our lives reading. What set

Ruth apart was that she not only read but remembered everything, and crowed with delight at the memory of a particularly absurd passage in a nineteenth-century novel of manners or casually tossed down a quotation from one of Shakespeare's minor characters. We can all quote Hamlet or Lear, but few can quote Lucilius or the Duke of Albany. I first became aware of her phenomenal memory, another thing I envy her, the second time we met, when Ruth and her husband and I were talking about the books we were currently reading. After confessing my embarrassment at having never before read Darwin, I said I was reading *The Voyage of the Beagle*, whereupon Ruth remarked on the beauty of his description of the guanacos of Patagonia. When I asked, she said she'd read it a few decades before and had been struck by the graceful felicity of that passage. In almost five years and in countless conversations, I never found a book she hadn't read. And remembered.

Ruth was also fiercely intelligent, gifted with a fine mind that was honed by reading, thought, and disputation. Like many intelligent people, she had little patience with ignorance or stupidity, and like many people whose success is the result of genius and hard work, she felt no need to feign politeness when she found herself confronted by ignorance in any of its guises. I've read interviews with her in which the reporters have come away more than a little chilled by Ruth's manner, one even going so far as to write of her 'beady eyes' and describing her as someone

who 'bristled like a threatened porcupine'. This, the inter-
viewer later revealed, was from someone who had gone
to interview her after having read only one of her books.
Rather like going to talk to Maria Callas after having listening to her sing a few arias from *Norma* on disc, isn't it?

In 1986, Ruth went through a process of intellectual
cell division and began to write books under the pseudo-
nym of Barbara Vine, a name constructed from her own
middle name and her grandmother's maiden name. In
these books, she said, she hoped to free herself from the
rules imposed by the detective genre and thus allow herself scope for greater psychological penetration. Hence,
when discussing her work, fans and readers invariably
discuss whom they prefer, Ruth Rendell or Barbara Vine.
The differences between them can be seen in two books,
Ruth Rendell's *A Judgement in Stone* and Barbara Vine's
A Dark-Adapted Eye, the first of the Barbara Vine books.

A Judgement in Stone, published in the United States
in 1977, was her sixteenth novel. This might seem like a
large number, were it not that she wrote more than fifty.
In itself, the writing of fifty books is not remarkable, no
more so than writing fifty operas. The difference, as with
the music, is in the quality, and the quality of her work
is remarkably and consistently high. There are books of
hers I like more than others, but that is an entirely sub-
jective matter. What does not change is the high level of
the prose, the unending invention, and, perhaps the thing

that most impresses me in her books, the depiction of character, at which she is supreme.

But all of this is the sort of vague generality I would not allow in a student paper. Let me turn my attention, instead, to the texts, for it is in them that her genius lies.

The opening sentence of *A Judgement in Stone* is: 'Eunice Parchman killed the Coverdale family because she could not read or write.' Well, there we have it: reason, crime, and killer all given to us in the opening sentence. Might as well toss the book aside, huh, and move on to the next? Nothing to discover? No question could be more absurd.

The next paragraph expands upon the motive: illiteracy is a deformity and will bring upon its victim nothing but shame and scorn. Should the illiterate person live in a world of the semi-literate, they can elude detection, but if they move into the world of the bookish, they are doomed to discovery and its resulting shame. Hence the tragedy that is to be visited upon the Coverdale family.

The bones of the plot are deceptively simple: Eunice Parchman is raised by a family that today would be called 'dysfunctional'. She is ignored, rather than abused, by her parents, and the result of that, a common theme in Rendell's work, is the creation of a monster who is not so much cut off from normal human emotions and responses as unaware of them, as a deaf person might be unaware of Bach or a blind person unfamiliar with Monet.

Utterly amoral and possessed of feral cunning, Eunice

observes the behaviour of her neighbours and discovers blackmail, almost as if she'd invented the possibility, and when her widowed father gets on her nerves, she discovers patricide. An orphan, then, she must find employment, and this she does as a maid in the home of the good and kindly Coverdales: George, a successful businessman; his second wife, Jacqueline; her son by her first marriage, Giles; and Miranda, George's daughter by his.

The Coverdales are bright, articulate, literate people who can remark upon a singer's failure to sing an ascending seventh in a Mozart aria and who quote passages from books back and forth in the accustomed code of the profoundly literate. Their literacy as well as their sympathy for the less fortunate are to prove their tragic flaws, for Eunice fears and abhors the printed word with the same instinctive loathing most people feel toward spiders, and their discovery of her illiteracy, the secret she has harboured and protected all her life, seals their fate.

The tragedy, however, needs a sparking element, and this is provided by Joan Smith, a village shopkeeper who enters the book in the first stages of a religious mania that grows steadily wilder until it reaches its climax with the all but ritual slaughter of the Coverdales.

Joan and Eunice join forces early in the book and quickly become a macabre Laurel and Hardy. Though both of them are strange-looking, Joan is the bizarre one. 'Joan Smith's coiffure, wiry, stiff, glittering, had the look of one of the yellow metal pot scourers displayed for sale on her shelves.' Once a whore, she abandoned the profession but kept the uniform and dresses her body, 'thin as a starved bird', in short, tight skirts and garish sweaters. Of Joan Smith's childlessness, the narrator observes, 'One wonders what Joan Smith would have done with children had she had any. Eaten them, perhaps.'

A character who might have been well advised to emulate Joan's childless state is Oedipus, and it is, yes, *Oedipus Rex* that comes to mind when I reflect upon Rendell's novel. Before the educated reader accuses me of either taking leave of my senses or of being in the pay of Baroness Rendell, let me point out that the similarities I observe reside in the prevailing mood and narrative technique more than in anything else. Even the first spectators at the Greek play knew what was going to happen to Oedipus and Jocasta, knew the horror that waited for them with the return of the shepherd, for they were familiar with the legend of Oedipus. Hence they could watch, with mounting horror, the way Oedipus wrapped around himself the fatal net that would destroy him. In the moment after Jocasta realizes what has happened, Oedipus can still say of himself, 'I am a child of Luck.' In one desperate, final attempt to avert what she now realizes is the inevitable tragedy, Jocasta implores her son/husband, 'Forget this herdsman. Forget it all. This talk is a waste of time.'

But Oedipus, blinded by pride and by the noble desire to be of help to his suffering city, refuses to heed the voice of warning and plunges ahead to his doom.

So, too, do the Coverdales spurn the repeated warnings of the danger that lies ahead of them. Wilfully, they choose to ignore or deny the signs of malice and inhumanity in their housemaid and reject every opportunity to rid themselves of her while we, the silent spectators to their fate, sit, hands pressed to whitened lips in horror at the inescapable consequences of their choices.

Sophocles puts his warnings into the mouths of the characters: as this is a play, he has no other choice. Rendell instead puts hers into the mouth of her narrator, and it is this Olympian voice that fascinates me. It is the narrator who tells us, from the first line, what is going to happen. It is the same narrator who tells us, time and time again, that *this* was the point where a decision might have been made that would have led to life and light. Rendell's debt to Thomas Hardy is evident here. Another of the many pleasures offered by this book is the fact that it is written for profoundly literate readers like the Coverdales. The language of Shakespeare, the Bible, and Dickens reverberates through the pages: how fitting for these people that the teller of their tale should speak in such a richly literate manner.

Barbara Vine's *A Dark-Adapted Eye* is narrated by one of the people involved peripherally in the tragedy, a niece of the killer. The book opens in a casual, offhand manner: 'On the morning Vera died I woke up very early.' Here is the narrative voice that will continue through the book: confiding, forthright, analytic, and intelligent. Faith Severn is the niece of Vera Hillyard, one of the last women to be hanged for murder in England. Thirty years before, she stabbed another woman to death, and now, prompted by questions from an investigative journalist who wants to make sense of the crime, Faith attempts to do the same.

The manipulation of chronology here is masterful, for Faith begins with the day of Vera's execution, and then, in order to begin to explain that to the reader, must retreat to events prior to that. In a way, it's rather like a grammatical exercise that attempts to explain the difference between the simple past tense and the past perfect in English: 'If a completed action took place before some other event in the past, then the past perfect must be used.' Unfortunately, the past is far from perfect in this book.

The chief events took place in the late 1940s, in those grim post-war years when rationing still had a fierce grip on England, and the remnants of an antiquated morality had a similarly fierce grip upon people's lives. The main character, Vera Longley, belongs to a type frequently found in the fiction of both Ruth Rendell and Barbara Vine: the repressed female who has been rigorously trained never, ever to raise her voice or make an outright display of any unpleasant emotion. Following some demented rule of female 'propriety', these women become domestic terrorists, black holes into which all thought of joy or ease is sucked. Like many of them, she proves capable of devotion to only a few people. In Vera's case, it is to her younger sister, Eden, and, eventually, to her son, Jamie.

As the narrator tells this discursive tale, winding back and forth, crossing her own trail like a serpent, referring with the ease of familiarity to characters the reader has never heard of or jumping wildly about in time, the reader is gradually forced to piece it all together: Vera gave birth to a baby who could not be her husband's, or perhaps the unmarried Eden gave birth to a baby and Vera agreed to claim it as her own, willing, for love of her sister, to take her shame upon herself. All would have been well, and Vera and her beloved Jamie would have continued to live in blissful poverty, were it not that Eden eventually married a millionaire and, finding herself unable to bear children, lay claim to the five-year-old child.

The secret that is kept here is not the name of the murderer: we know from the first pages that it was Vera. What is kept hidden from us for hundreds of pages is the name of the victim. And though we come to know the motive, we are never to learn the facts.

Both Eunice Parchman and Vera Hillyard are twisted in their emotions. Eunice is emotionally autistic and is seldom capable of feeling anything stronger than a mild irritation; because she lacks an emotional spectrum, she is trapped between white and black, and so the only possible step beyond irritation is homicidal rage. Vera is cursed in a similar way: usually vaguely displeased by whatever happens to her, she has reserved her love for only two people, her sister and her son. Because she, too, has no outlet for emotions on the normal scale, her love knows no limits and is manifest only in extremes. Unfortunately, self-sacrifice and murder are two of those manifestations.

Ruth Rendell, the cerebral Ruth, gives us a narrator who maintains throughout an Olympian vision of the characters; that distant, aloof voice never commits itself to sympathy, but its telling of the facts chills our hearts. Barbara Vine, on the other hand, gives us a narrator whose life was profoundly damaged by Vera's crime: her parents were led to a bleak separation, she herself to a doomed marriage and the failed promise of a bright future. Yet as she speaks to us and unfolds this tale of grim horror, her voice is never devoid of pity for Vera, and it is this pity that infects us. Vera was short-tempered and impatient, not very bright and utterly without humour. But, in the face of all-sacrificing love, what do those things matter? The narrator ends as confused as she begins, not really understanding the past and profoundly suspicious of the tricks memory plays upon us all.

And the voice behind these narrative voices, the *real* voice of Baroness Ruth Rendell, if a writer can be said to possess such a thing? Perhaps it is audible in her letters, for Ruth was a gifted and passionate letter-writer, and over the years I received more than my fair share of them. In them, she was, as she often was in her books, very, very funny. She had little patience, though a great deal of compassion, for the foibles of the world. She read and talked about books: histories of London, of the Plague, books by Henry James and Jane Austen. In short, she read. Everything.

And she listened. To Handel, as it turned out. In one of her last letters, she remarked upon her first hearing of the oratorio *Saul*: 'Wonderful, yes, and one has to hear the celebrated Dead March in context fully to appreciate it. I am definitely going to have it at my funeral or perhaps at my memorial service. Do come.'

A Complex Character

Never underestimate the possibility of coincidence. Each year, I set aside a Real Book for summer reading: usually one of the Classics; this summer it is the *Aeneid*, which I've not read in half a century. No sooner had I read it than I was asked to write about Berlioz's *Les Troyens*, and in this offer – as would a pious Roman matron – I saw the Hand of Fate, for it provided me a chance to say high-minded, Serious-Sounding things about culture.

With the rich complexity of Virgil's text still in my mind, I was struck by the fact that an opera libretto contains only the words the characters sing – the emotional thrust is conveyed by the music and the singing – while in a narrative poem, the poet's voice explains the subtle shift in the emotions of the characters and lends them a certain credibility because convention requires that we believe the narrator.

The books in the *Aeneid* in which Dido is mentioned provide an example of narrative interference (if you will). The narrator repeatedly refers to the hero as 'pious' and 'dutiful', hardly virtues that allow for operatic virtuosity. Virgil wishes to sum up the man and provide an explanation for his single-minded dedication to a city he has yet to see: could there have been a loftier subject for a writer of Virgil's times than the founding of Rome? Aeneas is, after all, the divinely commanded founder of the city that was to rule the world and the hero of the greatest Roman epic: he had thus to be presented in a flattering light and as an admirable, virtuous figure. He has little choice but to leave Dido, for his mission is to found the world-conquering city-state of Rome. To persuade us that he did this from duty and not from whim, the narrator of the poem tells us that Aeneas still 'desired to ease her sadness by comforting her and to turn away pain'.

The lack of a narrator makes it possible to view Berlioz's Aeneas as an entirely different sort of man. When he is preparing to sneak away from Carthage without bothering to bid his lover farewell, and is caught at it by Dido, the best he can do is whine, '*En ma douleur profonde,/ Chère Didon, épargnez-moi!*' When it's clear that Dido isn't buying this one, he explains – sounding rather like a Jehovah's Witness caught sneaking out of a bar – that he is under the power of '*des dieux les ordres souverains*'. Furthermore, he's capable of telling Dido that he is '*digne de ton pardon*' (doesn't the victim usually get to decide this one?), thus remaining both self-centred and self-deceiving until Dido leaves him to go to her death.

Without a narrator to present his case, Aeneas is at the mercy of any stage director who wants to present him as a weakling or a cad: the paragraph above is an example of what mischief they can get up to in the absence of a narrator to protect Aeneas from their 'concept'. One can but hope that the passionate sincerity of Aeneas' last aria would resist this sort of directorial interference.

Berlioz's Dido, poor goose, loves him to the point of madness even as she climbs to the top of what is to be her funeral pyre and kills herself. '*Oh! Mon âme te suit/A son amour enchaînée.*' Her last direct reference to Aeneas is her prayer to his mother, '*Vénus! Rends-moi ton fils!*' These, at least in the nineteenth century, were the proper words for a woman to sing while killing herself for love, especially if she was using her lover's sword to do it.

Virgil, a man with a Roman sense of decorum, warns his reader that Dido's love for Aeneas 'weakens her sense of shame' because 'her tender marrow is aflame'. As to the power of the gods, 'What use are prayers and shrines to the impassioned?' All that is left to her is lust for vengeance. Before she kills herself, she curses Aeneas and wishes him this: 'Let him beg help and watch the shameful death of his people . . . Let him die before his time, and lie unburied on the sand.'

Since Virgil was also explaining to his readers the historical antipathy between Rome and Carthage, his heroine curses not only her lover but his entire race: 'O Tyrians, pursue my hatred against his whole line and the race to come . . . Let there be no love or treaties between our peoples.'

Virgil's goal was political as well as artistic; Dido was,

after all, the Queen of Carthage, that city bold enough to have rivalled the power of Rome. It had to be destroyed, like Dido, to allow for the eventual triumph of the new capital of the world.

Berlioz, a man of his times, and an opera composer as well, cares not a whit for the glory of Rome, nor for historical accuracy. He wants a grandiose, romantic heroine who will sing gloriously until she drops, a victim not of politics or the interfering gods but of love, love, love.

Love

Dear Guido

Dear Guido,

Well, here we are, more than thirty years later, and still together. I'm happy to have helped you meet so many interesting people over the years and do apologize for the fact that many of them surprised you by turning out to be criminals and liars. I hope there were enough good people as well to make up for the villains.

I've managed to keep your kids away from drugs and bad company, at least this far. And your daughter's interest in ecology is certainly something you, and she, can be proud of.

I've given you a wife who, although a bit of a snob, is still amusing and supportive. And she's a fabulous cook, so please continue to appreciate her as much as you do.

I've also passed on to you the books I was reading while writing the novels, so that you could read them too. And even though I adore baroque opera, I have not made you go to the opera more than two or three times.

You've also changed your thoughts on some things. Remember when you treated climate change as a joke and called your kids 'the Water Police' for making you take short showers? Well, you're a convert and a believer now, aren't you, after seeing the things you've seen in many of the novels about the way the Earth is being polluted and harmed?

And, at long last, although it took me thirty books to do it, I finally pointed out how strong and stupid is your prejudice against Southerners. I'm relieved that you saw the truth of it and were ashamed to realize how invisible your prejudice had been to you all your life.

It's been a great time together, my dearest Guido, and I hope it means we are together for life.

Love,
Donna

Gardening

My mother, the spirit of truth forces me to write, was a dirty woman. Yes, my own dear, sainted, half-Irish mother. Dirty, dirty, dirty. If I think of her, I see her in Bermuda shorts but with dirty knees. One might even say her knees were filthy, pieces of grass sticking to them, occasionally a squashed rose hip. Best to pass over the actual shorts in silence, or perhaps with a deep sigh. In a better class of home than the one in which I was raised, they would have been given to charity or the cleaning lady, though washed first. Or perhaps they would have been thrown away or taken out to the back of the house and burned.

Her hands were roughed by work, the nails broken, very often with deposits of dirt underneath. I remember seeing her scrubbing at them with a succession of nail brushes, but nothing served to get rid of the dirt, at least not before the onset of winter.

For my mother, you see, was a passionate gardener. She was a digger, a ripper-outer, a smasher of snails, and a saver of seeds. She was a transplanter, the keeper of a compost heap decades before they were fashionable, a friend to worms, an enemy to insects save for ladybugs, and – I blush to say this – a thief.

During my formative years, I watched this mild-mannered and always polite and soft-spoken woman sneak into the gardens of her unsuspecting victims to snatch up deadheaded flowers from the ground. I watched countless times as she waited for her friends to turn their backs, when she would stuff a dried-out flower in the pocket of her skirt; only when safe at home would she remove it and shake out the seeds on a sheet of newspaper to dry and save for spring planting.

My mother was also an assassin. Countless times I watched her stalk through her enormous garden, in one hand an empty tin can from the various and consistently dreadful tinned vegetables the family ate (vegetables grew in cans; my mother grew flowers), plucking Japanese beetles from the leaves of her flowers and dropping them into an inch of gasoline. She dealt out a similar fate to the aphids she found on the roses, plucking them from the stems with a tiny paintbrush repeatedly dipped into a can of water and liquid dish soap.

She seemed to believe that all public land belonged to her, a fact that gave her the right to pull the car to the side of any road alongside which grew a flower she wanted: thus she gave a home to poppies, sun-flowers, irises (in this case, she had to remember where they were and return later in the year to dig up the bulbs), asters and buttercups – and these are only the ones I remember from the looting expeditions into which she dragooned me. Luckily, my absence from her solo raids spares my conscience the knowledge of what she got up to on her own.

Once, when I was staying with my parents as an adult, she woke me in the dead of night, saying that we had to go and save Harry's manure pile. Harry, a friend of her father, and like him a farmer, had died, and his family had sold his farm to property developers. That very morning, my mother told me in shocked tones, the Caterpillars and backhoes were coming to level the property, and that meant the sixty-year-old manure pile would be destroyed. Why is it that I didn't even think of arguing with her, of telling her that three o'clock was not the proper time to go out to steal – in a word – horseshit?

We got in the car, the trunk filled, unbeknownst to me, with empty feedbags and some large plastic buckets, and off we went. She had put two shovels and two pairs of gardening gloves in with the sacks, thus we had little trouble in filling them and the buckets. We opened the windows of the car.

The time came for rosy-fingered dawn to grace us with her arrival. I was far more concerned about the arrival of the police. My mother, blithely undisturbed, said that we also had to save the violets 'before it's too late'. Too late to call a lawyer? Too late to remove the pyjamas I was wearing under my clothing? Too late to walk away and let her be arrested alone? But pause, gentle reader: she was my white-haired, half-Irish mother, and could I leave her to the mercies of the law?

So we started to save the violets – since it was May – before they would wither. Packing them into the car kept her happily occupied until we decided the car could hold no more and drove home. The violets, I remember, were still planted in the back garden when she died, and I hope they're still there now.

A Book of a Lifetime

One of the miraculous qualities of great books is the chameleon-like changes that take place in them during a lifetime of reading. Read *Pride and Prejudice* as a teenager and delight in the love story between charming, outspoken Lizzy and arrogant, overbearing Mr Darcy.

Like a foxhound being trained to detect only the scent of the fox, a young reader will pick up the aroma of love, love, love and follow it right through to the end. There is the instant attraction between Lizzy and Darcy, denied by both, the sparring, the dancing together, the wit, the umbrage, and the final realization that this is the one person upon whom a throbbing heart can safely be bestowed.

Yes, it is about love, but sometime later in life the reader realizes it is also about the love that comes from resignation, seen when Charlotte Lucas accepts the offer of the unspeakable, plodding Mr Collins. She knows she is not young, and she is poor; she knows she is not a catch, and so she will accept Mr Collins's proposal and love him until death do them part. Mr Bennet is mildly concerned for his daughters' futures and puts up with his wife: it's as close to love as this disappointed man can come, the best he can give. Lady Catherine probably loves her daughter, poor thing.

To read the book a half-century later is also to see how overwhelmingly the book is about money. Every man has his worth, and it is expressed in pounds per year. Mr Darcy is thus worth more than his friend Mr Bingley, and, indeed, he gets the sparkling Lizzy and Mr Bingley gets the sober, even-headed Jane. And Mr Collins, who is not worth as much as either one of them, gets Charlotte Lucas. Frivolous – not to use a stronger word – Lydia gets Wickham, who has to be paid off to have her.

Lizzy and Jane and their sisters are pretty much – I don't like having to say it – worthless. No dowry, father's house entailed, no education, not even enough to enable them to be governesses: without the arrival of Darcy and Bingley, what would await them?

What woman is worth the most? Lady Catherine's listless, ailing daughter, Anne. One of the comforts of age is that even this grim knowledge of social reality does nothing to diminish the sparkle of life that fills every page of this most glorious of novels, and so the reading of it is a lifelong joy.

Moment of Truth

The Death of Ivan Ilyich

Many of us who are readers by habit look at the summer as a time to cheat: we get to eat too much ice cream, spend too much time lolling about in the sun, gain a few kilos, and allow ourselves to consume a few junk books along with the ice cream. If we're lucky, we get invited to someone's summer house on a lake, where, accompanied by that damp, musty smell that seems to occur only in old houses by lakes, we can glance through their books and, taking a high moral tone, sneak a look at the biography of Michael Jackson and, if caught, always say we just wanted to take a look at the photos. Or we can reread *The Scarlet Pimpernel*, *The Wind in the Willows* or even *Gone with the Wind* with a clear conscience: after all, it's the summer, isn't it?

Occasionally, however, tumbled to one side on those same shelves is a real book that grabs our attention by the throat and reminds us of what books really can do for us. It was my good fortune one summer some years ago, amidst the ice cream, and occasionally afloat, to have the opportunity to reread Tolstoy's *The Death of Ivan Ilych*, a book I hadn't read for at least ten years, though it is one that Gore Vidal, I think it was, dismissed as being tediously didactic.

This is what happens. 'A successful, married government functionary, in the process of decorating his fashionable new home, hurts himself in a stupid accident and then, cared for by his loyal servant Gerasim, dies.' But the tricky aspects unfold as soon as you have a look at the adjectives.

Successful. By all common standards, Ivan Ilyich is a successful man. He's a judge, one who has risen up through the ranks of the magistracy by dint of perseverance, connections, and string-pulling until he achieves his goal of a post two places above his colleagues and with a considerable rise in salary. As the nagging pain in his side worsens and inactivity leads to reflection, he comes to realize that one of the things he most enjoyed about his job was the exercise of power, the sense that, with a command or a look, he could cow another man into trembling silence. Somehow, he realizes, this really wasn't what he wanted to do with his life.

Married. He has married Praskovya Fyodorovna, a woman for whom he felt a strong initial attraction – besides, she was of the right class, and, furthermore, she was there, and it was the right time for a man of his position to think of marriage. They fight. They have little in common. They've been together decades, and after his death she has this to say of his last agony: 'I can't understand how I endured it. It could be heard through three doors. Ah! What I have endured.'

Fashionable. The narrator makes it clear that this last house of Ivan Ilych, the house in which, and for which, he will die, possesses 'just what is usually seen in the homes of people of moderate means who want to appear rich, and therefore succeed only in resembling others like themselves.' His life, Ivan Ilych comes to see during his last agony, has been identical to the lives of the people living in those houses.

Stupid. He injures himself while hanging the curtains, gives himself a whack on the side that, with the passage of time, will cause his death. He dies for his drapes.

Loyal. Gerasim is the only person who treats Ivan Ilych with anything more than irritated impatience. His doctors poke and prod, diagnose this and that, prescribe medicines of varying degrees of uselessness while encouraging in him the illusion that there is hope, and never fail to be paid. His wife and daughter stop in to visit the sickroom on their way out to various entertainments and join in the collective fiction that he is not dying. Only Gerasim, the stoic, kind peasant, sees no reason to hide the truth from his master: 'We shall all come to it some day.'

And that's it. Sort of. After his months of suffering, after his final hours of agony, Ivan Ilych looks back upon his life and sees how he has tossed it away for nothing, following the chimera of 'fashion' or 'propriety' and leaving behind him a trail of stupid and worthless choices. At the end, illusion blasted away by pain and the inescapable realization that he will die, he sees that he has lived his life according to rules set for him by strangers and in the hope of making some sort of impression upon those strangers. He has spent his life with a woman he doesn't like, had two children for whom he feels no special fondness, worked in a job he realizes wasn't what he wanted to do. And always, always, his choices have been nonchoices; he was no more in charge of what he did than a proboscis monkey when it chooses a mate because of the size and colour of its nose.

In one of his works, Aristotle remarks that one glimpse of what he calls 'celestial isness' gives us more joy than all the world. Whatever truth Ivan Ilych perceives during his final epiphany, whether it is celestial isness or some glimpse that there is light after his wasted life, his illumination leads him to joy and a sense that death is finished.

It is impossible to read this novella without shivering at how much it reflects our times. And us. But, lest another Gore Vidal come upon these words, I shall not belabour that point.

The Big Bow Wow

If you promise to do a thing, then you must do it, right? No matter the cost in time or energy, you've committed yourself, so you have no choice in the matter. When the publishing house in which Sir Walter Scott was a partner declared bankruptcy in 1825, he refused to escape personal responsibility by declaring himself bankrupt and thus condemned himself to a lifetime of writing novels to pay off the debts incurred by other people's incompetence. But he had given his word.

It is this principle that animated me when the Semper Opera came tapping at my email not too long ago, reminding me that I'd given my word to write something about *Lucia di Lammermoor*. If Scott could write the novel, I could certainly write a short article. Besides, it would give me the chance to consider again a book I'd not read since university. His historical novels were still assigned texts, though his writing and sensibility had even then begun to pass out of fashion.

I've always admired Scott, not so much for his novels, three of which I'd had to read (much of academic life is spent reading the unreadable and then, worse, talking about it, and then, worse still, writing about it), but for his greatness of spirit and generosity. It was he who wrote of Jane Austen, a decade after her death: 'That young lady had a talent for describing the involvements and feelings and characters of ordinary life, which to me is the most wonderful I ever met with. The Big Bow Wow strain I can do myself like anyone now going, but the exquisite touch, which renders ordinary commonplace things and characters interesting, from the truth of the description and the sentiment, is denied to me. What a pity such a gifted creature died so early.'

Thus in his sober style he paid tribute to the writer beneath whom literary taste has now ranked him. He was not, however, to be outdone in graciousness and generosity by his literary colleague, Miss Austen herself, who wrote of her fantastically more famous colleague, 'Walter Scott has no business to write novels, especially good ones. – It is not fair. – He has Fame and Profit enough as a Poet, and should not be taking the bread out of other people's mouths. – I do not like him, do not mean to like *Waverley* if I can help it – but fear I must.'

How characteristic of these two writers these brief passages are. Scott refers to his 'Bow Wow strain', while Austen writes of not wanting to like his new novel but 'fears' she must. He uses boastful language but uses it to mock himself. She slips in one word – 'fear' – and turns her criticism into praise.

Well, yes, Sir Walter Scott could indeed Bow Wow

like anyone then going: this is one of the reasons *Lucia di Lammermoor*, which is based on his novel *The Bride of Lammermoor*, was transmuted into a great opera, for grand opera has to go 'Bow Wow', and if the final scene of *Lucia di Lammermoor* is not Bow-Wowing at its best, I'll do what one of Dickens's minor characters says and eat my head.

In the case of the opera, however, the Bow-Wowing is not Scott's but that of Salvadore Cammarano, who also did a lot more of it in the final scene of Donizetti's *Roberto Devereux*. Scott gave Cammarano precious little to work with, describing Lucy's behaviour after her wedding night thusly: 'Here they found the unfortunate girl seated, or rather couched like a hare upon its form – her head-gear dishevelled, her night-clothes torn and dabbled with blood, her eyes glazed, and her features convulsed into a wild paroxysm of insanity. When she saw herself discovered, she gibbered, made mouths, and pointed at them with her bloody fingers, with the frantic gestures of an exulting demoniac.'

Well, I've seen a number of sopranos sing Lucia, and not one of them gibbered, though all of them, to one degree or another, gave decidedly frantic paroxysms of insanity. Scott gave no further information, save that Lucy died, thus everything was left to the fiery imagination of Cammarano.

The operatic Lucia enters wearing her blood-splattered wedding dress, a costume choice equalled in creepiness only by the one Miss Havisham wears in *Great Expectations* and in which she, too, will die. Lucia has lost her mind and is sure in her madness that she is on the way to the altar to be united at last with her beloved Edgardo.

More importantly, Donizetti pulls out all the stops to write what is certainly one of the best-known scenes in opera. It might even be the maddest mad scene, though it's rather difficult to make a sane judgement here. Lucia sings, her joy in a snake-like embrace with her madness, and flirts vocally with two flutes (unless the opera company has a glass harmonica), tossing out and up a seemingly endless series of trills, runs, and cadenzas, until the music leads her up and up into the realm of complete madness and wonderfully operatic death.

> *Ah! L'inno*
> *suona di nozze! Il rito*
> *per noi s'appresta! . . . Oh me felice! . . .*
> *Edgardo, Edgardo, oh me felice!*
> *Oh, gioia che si sente e non si dice!*
> *Ardon gli incensi . . . splendon*
> *le sacre faci, splendon intorno!*
> *Ecco il Ministro! Porgimi*
> *La destra! . . . Oh, lieto giorno!*
> *Alfin son tua, alfin sei mio,*
> *a me ti dona un Dio.*

It's inevitable that Donizetti and Cammarano would create this unhinged scene. Opera, after all, has to *show* what is happening and thus allow the audience to *hear* its effects on and in the various characters. It's well enough for a novelist to name a 'wild paroxysm of insanity', but that doesn't tell a reader (or, for that matter, a stage director) what that looks and sounds like. Nor is the viewer and listener much helped by being told that the heroine 'gibbered' and 'made mouths'.

That is part of the reason we go to the opera. It's not enough to read the story, know the plot, know what happens in the end. We need the rush of blood to the head; we need the heart to go boom boom boom as those bewigged and crinolined women are either thrilled or disgusted by the declaration of love from the tenor or the baritone.

We need the pulse and power of the music that goes along with her emotions. In order for our own hearts to throb, we need more than to read it: we need to see it and we need to hear it, for only then will we be captured by art's biggest Bow Wow.

Show, Don't Tell

'Show, don't tell.' 'Show, don't tell.' How many teachers of creative writing have beaten their heads – and their students' heads – against the wall as they repeat this injunction? Cut down on the narrative explanations and let the action of the novel *show* what is happening. Don't tell the reader what a character is like: make that character *show* his soul with a revelatory gesture or word.

One pedagogical tactic that desperate teachers might employ is to direct the attention of their students to the novels of Ross Macdonald, for there are few better, more concrete examples of a writer who went quietly and artfully about the business of showing his readers the souls of his characters. Even more artfully, Macdonald kept authorial comment to a minimum while allowing the characters in his novels to strip themselves – or one another – bare with the words they hurled or simply let drop inattentively.

In the case of the crime novel, there is another professorial injunction that is much repeated: the plot must move like the flight of an arrow, always aiming at a single target. Of course, this arrow can be buffeted about by the winds of art or skill or craft and zig a bit in one direction or zag a bit in the other, but the plot should always be headed in one direction, towards the revelation of the motivation, and thus the perpetrator, of whatever crime the novel examines.

And here again Macdonald can serve as an example, for he is the William Tell of plotters. He's also a deft hand at zigging and zagging, but no matter what pirouettes or divagations his arrows make, and even if they take twenty years to get to the target, they always land smack in the smallest of those concentric circles.

Lit crit is filled with the most idle sort of speculation about the literary ancestors of writers, and all manner of progeny spring forth from the strangest of putative parents. Homer has become the grandfather of almost anyone who tells a linear story, and Proustian parthenogenesis is claimed for anyone who takes a look inside the heart or head of a character. In Macdonald's case, the family tree is firmly rooted in the novels of Charles Dickens, at least the part of the heritage that has to do with plotting. The solution to the mystery at the heart of *Bleak House* lies two decades in the past, and the identity of Pip's anonymous patron in *Great Expectations* is not revealed until the end of the book, and that too is linked to events in the distant past.

Macdonald begins his Lew Archer novels with a problem in the present – a missing heir, a contested will, a stolen heirloom – which he is hired to investigate, and the arrow of the plot, though aimed from the present into the future, is sure to flip around and start flying into the past, striking down victims as it goes. Back in time it streaks, a generation, two, until it strikes hard and fast in some event or person whose corrupting shadow will be shown to loom over the present. Think of Goya at his bleakest – a father devouring his progeny, the hands of the innocent thrown up in a useless attempt to prevent death – and you have an idea of what Lew Archer's investigations will turn up. 'I had handled cases which opened up gradually like fissures in the firm ground of the present, cleaving far down through the strata of the past' (*The Chill*, 1963). In novel after novel, some person in the present asks Archer to look into a problem, hoping that the future will thus become more secure. But almost invariably, the first domino falls in the opposite direction, and the book sweeps into the past, knocking down reputations and old truths. Very quickly, the future is infected by the scent of death emanating from those unlocked secrets, and bodies begin to pile up.

There being so many, it is difficult to single out Ross Macdonald's masterpiece, but *The Blue Hammer* certainly comes as close as any. Hired by a wealthy woman to investigate the disappearance of a painting from her home, Archer drives up a private road to speak to the owners, Jack and Ruth Biemeyer, and finds them on the court behind their sprawling home, playing tennis like 'prisoners in an exercise yard'.

When Archer explains that he is late because he had 'some trouble finding your road,' Jack Biemeyer tells him he could have asked anybody in town because 'Everybody knows where Jack Biemeyer lives. Even the planes coming in use my home as a landmark.'

Show the location, *show* the location, the huddled students are told. Well, how's this for showing? 'We trekked to the far side of a big central room.' Then there is Mrs Biemeyer's explanation for her delay in noticing the absence of the painting: 'I don't come into this room every day.' Just in case Archer hasn't grasped the wealth of the people who are going to hire him, Biemeyer laments that 'There ought to be some place in a four-hundred-thousand-dollar building where a man can sit down in peace.' This in 1976, when that sum bought a lot more house than it does today. And notice that Biemeyer refers to his own home as a 'building'.

Archer is asked to try to find the painting, which resembles the work of Richard Chantry, a famous local painter who disappeared more than two decades before. The Biemeyers' daughter is involved in some way with Fred Johnson, a no-longer-young student at the nearby college, who is passionately interested in Chantry's work.

And there we have it: the classic Ross Macdonald take-off. A young woman is perceived to be in jeopardy, her young man has questionable motives for his interest in her, and the hands of the clock have been turned back a generation. The more Archer tries to make sense of the present, the more the grasping hands of the past reach out to pull him backwards, and the more evident it becomes that remote events are the real causes of what happens in the book.

Soon Archer stumbles on the first murder victim, who mutters Chantry's name before dying. But if Chantry is correctly presumed to be dead these many years, why is a dying man naming him, and how can this man have sold what might be a recently painted Chantry?

The woman in the painting is identified as Mildred Mead, a woman over whom men fought decades before. Her presence, image, and absence haunt the book, and her raw sexual appeal is felt by most of the male characters, including Archer, who has the attractive quality of responding to and appreciating women. When he meets a young woman journalist, 'Her passage left vibrations on the air. The vibrations lingered in my body.' Those vibrations pass between them both, and it is not long before they are checking into the same hotel room. The manner in which Archer presents his interest in women might today be seen as curiously old-fashioned, though one wonders when admiration, affection, and protective love went out of fashion. In the tradition of the Golden Age of crime writing, Macdonald mentions sexual activity but does not describe it.

Archer – no zealot in search of social justice, no crusader in defence of the oppressed – occasionally reveals the ethical underpinnings of his life and work: 'There were pairs of lovers here and there in the grass instead of dead men, and that was good.' He speaks of his failed marriage with constant regret and blames himself entirely for its failure. He writes of people, even the bad, with the compassion that comes of an understanding of human weakness, and his sympathy for the people life has turned into failures is bottomless. His contempt for the powerful and arrogant is clear, though here, as well, he allows them to dig their own graves; he *shows* them as they are, rendering comment superfluous. Jack Biemeyer, told that 'A woman's life may be at stake,' responds only, 'People die every day.' It is not always heartlessness that the characters inadvertently reveal. A hard-nosed policeman, speaking of the failure of homosexuals to stay the course of life, surprises Archer by relenting, adding, 'And they have a tougher course to run than most of us.'

As in Dickens, Macdonald's chickens always come home to roost. Though the villains kill and maim in their attempt to keep their secrets hidden, once Archer has started to poke around in the past, facts come to light, leading to surmises, connections, and ultimately to revelation.

Sustaining this is prose so elegant and rich as to drive any writer to fits of envy. Every page contains a turn of phrase that is beyond imitation, a simile beyond praise. Young policemen wear 'light summery clothes and dark wintry faces'. 'Her eyes brightened with interest, and with the superiority that liars feel towards the people they lie to.' After a party, 'the room was like a visible hangover'.

'Both physically and emotionally, I thought, she was a bit dilapidated.' 'The sunset spread across the sea like a conflagration so intense that it fed on water.' Almost any page of the Archer novels contains an example of this authorial largesse. *The Chill* is filled with them: 'A young man with an untrimmed beard and rebellious eyes looked like a conscientious objector to everything.' 'Her hair was dyed black, with a greenish sheen on it like certain ducks.' 'Kincaid was a frightened man who valued his status the way some previous generations valued their souls.' How strong is the temptation to steal phrases from him. The prose, alas, is so distinctively his own, the theft would be too easily traced and Lew Archer would solve the case in a moment.

How rare and how refreshing, in this age of crime novels filled with graphic descriptions of sex and violence and with autopsies that run on for pages, to find a writer who, like the Greeks, prefers to keep the violence offstage and whose interest is not in the violence itself but in understanding what brought it about and how it has blighted the lives of all those touched by it.

The Blue Hammer, like the other Archer novels, grows more complicated as the plot unfolds and Archer becomes ever more driven to learn what might have happened, and why. Each new discovery leads to another, and many of them lead to murder. A man is drowned, a long-dead body is unearthed, and different people turn out not to be who they appear to be, or were. Archer moves doggedly forward, driven by his desire to understand past and present events as well as by his compassion for the people haunted and destroyed by those events. In the final pages of the book, the whole wretched fabric of jealousy, spite, and a twisted combination of terror and possessiveness that calls itself love is ripped to tatters, revealing the monstrous forms into which human weakness can be moulded. Archer – who has served, however inadvertently, as an avenging angel in the book – can view what remains only with pity. Such is Macdonald's brilliance as a writer that the reader is lured into feeling the same emotion.

Ends

The Big Sleep

Raymond Chandler once wrote that 'The emotional basis of the standard detective story was and had always been that murder will out and justice will be done.' However astute he might have been in describing them, Chandler chose not to play by these rules. To hell with the ordered, enclosed world of Agatha Christie's novels, where crime was an aberration and the task of the investigator was to discover and banish the malefactor so that the peaceful harmony of the quiet, enclosed world could be returned to its pre-crime state. Before Chandler got his hands on it, the detective novel played by unwritten rules: a single perpetrator was responsible for the aberrant behaviour; once the perpetrator was unmasked, he or she was rendered powerless and the existing order was restored. The essential point was that the return of social order was both possible and desirable.

Chandler was having none of this; he didn't believe it was possible, anyway. The society in which his books take place is neither ordered nor law-abiding. Instead, it is a dark sea in which predators eat prey. Nothing can stop them from doing so, for this is the new social order.

The society Chandler describes in his novels is corrupt in every way. In his first and most famous novel, *The Big Sleep*, there is no chance that the revelation of the identity of the criminal, even his or her arrest, will change anything. If those who make and enforce the laws are equally corrupt, then the possibility of justice is excluded a priori. The detective, no matter how well intentioned, will never eliminate, not even limit, evil or crime. This inevitable defeat leads to a pervasive sense of individual despair, social chaos, and the triumph of evil. Christie's country-house murders end with a return to innocence; this is impossible in Chandler's world, where there is no innocence to return to.

This is the world in which Chandler's detective, Philip Marlowe, lives and works; and suffers. This is the world of *The Big Sleep*.

A wealthy old man, General Sternwood, aware that death is hastening closer, asks private detective Philip Marlowe, the protagonist – it's hard to call him the hero – to deal with a blackmailer who is threatening his dissolute daughter, Carmen, and stop her from getting into even more serious trouble. Their meeting takes place in a claustrophobic hothouse filled with orchids that resemble 'the newly washed fingers of dead men'. The setting prefigures the entire novel, which takes place in an equally overheated world that, like the orchids, is nourished by decomposing bodies. We are made aware of the similarity between plants and humans. The General's hair 'clung to his scalp like wild flowers fighting for life on a bare rock.' The hothouse feels and smells corrupt; the General's daughters have the same scent.

The blackmailer has some photographs of Carmen in a more-than-compromising situation. Remember, the book comes from an era when this was possible, when people did not willingly immortalize their sexual activities on Facebook. Marlowe, with some reluctance, accepts the quest, although he soon realizes there is little he can do – indeed, anyone can do – to save Carmen. His attempt to retrieve and destroy the photographs leads him – as happened to many knights errant in former times – into a maze of surprise and danger, to events that are prefigured by the stained-glass panel on the Sternwoods' door showing 'a knight in dark armor rescuing a lady who was tied to a tree and didn't have any clothes on but some very long and convenient hair.' Soon, people involved with Marlowe's expanding investigation, even in seemingly minor ways, begin to be murdered, their deaths apparently related to Carmen.

While trying to help the General's younger daughter, Marlowe meets and is attracted to her older sister, Vivian, who at first seems less reckless than her sister, though her past is chequered with indiscretion and excess. Her husband, Rusty Regan, seems to have run off with the wife of a well-known criminal, Eddie Mars. As the novel progresses, so does Marlowe's interest in her.

Marlowe's first move is to find the blackmailer, but

almost as soon as he finds the man's home, Marlowe hears three shots. When he breaks in – 'About the only part of a California house you can't put your foot through is the front door' – he hears footsteps disappearing down the back staircase, and sees a dead man at his feet, a naked and drugged Carmen giggling and unaware of what is going on. This murder is to prove only the first in a long series that runs like a thread through the book as more and more people are eliminated before Marlowe can get any clear information from them.

Like an insect not at first noticed on the leaf of an orchid, the disappearance of Rusty Regan suddenly comes into closer view, and the novel veers off into a new world. Because General Sternwood holds Regan in great regard, Marlowe – the knight errant – goes off in pursuit of him.

His quest leads him into far more dangerous territory, for he enters the violent world of Eddie Mars, whom Marlowe describes as 'a pornographer, a blackmailer, a hot car broker, a killer by remote control, and a suborner of crooked cops.' Even knowing these things about Mars does not prepare him for the monsters who inhabit his world, chief among them Lash Canino, his paid killer.

Strangely, even though both of the worlds he investigates show Marlowe little more than variations on the theme of human weakness and corruption, he cannot free himself from a belief in the goodness of women; well, of some women. Not only is he attracted to Vivian Sternwood, but he finds himself convinced of the goodness of

Eddie Mars's wife, Mona, whom he idealizes in a manner reminiscent of the conventions of Courtly Love.

Marlowe comes, by the end of the book, to understand fully what has happened, both to Carmen and to Rusty Regan. To his greater cost, he cannot any longer deceive himself about the way both of the women he has admired, and perhaps desired, were affected – and infected – by the world in which they live.

At the end, he has learned a great deal about the characters and their crimes, but he has also learned to ask, 'What did it matter where you lay once you were dead? . . . You just slept the big sleep, not caring about the nastiness of how you died or where you fell.' He has led his readers a long way from the bucolic somnolence of Agatha Christie's quiet little village.

Loneliness

At first, the idea of having a medical conference where I would speak about loneliness seemed strange. Just think of the last twenty minutes of your own life: chatting with friends, being introduced to people you've wanted to meet, asked about your own new projects, explaining progress in your research, being in a room of healthy people with jobs, families, interests, hobbies, books to read, movies to watch, places to go, things to *do*. We're too busy to be lonely, aren't we?

Many things about loneliness are unusual. The first that struck me was its resemblance to venereal disease. People who think they might have either problem are often reluctant to go to a doctor and – get ready for the next word – confess the name of the disease they think they might have. The reason for this timidity, this embarrassment, comes, I think, from loneliness's bad reputation: only losers are lonely, which I think would be a great title for a country and western song – 'I'm only a lonely cowboy, got only my cows to love.'

I was also struck by the fact that the 'lonely' person in the country and western tradition is almost always a male: 'lonesome cowboy', 'lonely rider', 'lone wolf'. From available statistics, however, this does not seem to be the case: recent surveys suggest that men and women suffer equally from loneliness, although men appear to be more reluctant to seek medical help.

I remain incapable of finding the right word to use when speaking of a person's loneliness. Does one 'get' loneliness, or 'have' loneliness? Does it grow on a person? Or can we talk about it only by saying that someone is 'suffering from' it? For they certainly do suffer.

Language reflects significant differences in attitudes towards loneliness. English has two words: loneliness and solitude. Loneliness is unquestionably bad and a source of suffering, for the word strongly suggests the lack of friends, or the solace of human company. Solitude, however, is neutral and refers to the situation in which a person lives alone by choice. The word also legitimizes the choice of solitude and the pleasure that can be taken in being alone. Well, it *is* an English word, isn't it?

Then what about 'solitary confinement', those weasel words so popular among people who run prisons. 'Solitary'. OK, that's clear enough: the person is alone. The 'confinement', however, refers to a metal box that usually measures two by three metres. Alone. What strikes me here is the way this description of what is in fact torture is meant to be softened by the name given to it, suggestive as it is of a suite at the nearest Kempinski hotel.

The Italians, bless them, have only one word, *'soli-tudine'*, and it does not name a situation that Italians think is pleasant. To the best of my knowledge, the Italians have no neutral word to describe being alone – *'da solo'* is two words – which I see as a linguistic assertion of their dislike and suspicion of solitude, as though their vocabulary sniffed at the idea of a human being left alone for long periods of time and didn't much like the smell of it.

I've always wondered why they so often go on vacation in groups: perhaps the answer lies in the unquestionable unpleasantness of *solitudine*, even for a short vacation.

Many writers have shown what loneliness can be but never has loneliness inside a – unhappy – marriage been dealt with more dreadfully than in Tolstoy's 1886 novella *The Death of Ivan Ilych*. When his widow is asked if her husband suffered before dying, she says: 'For three days in a row he screamed incessantly. It was unbearable. I can't understand how I endured it. It could be heard through three doors. Ah! What I have endured.'

I recall a scene from a children's book I read many years ago in which the animals go in search of something, but 'the more they looked, the more it wasn't there.' The opposite is true of recent medical interest in loneliness, for the more the doctors look, the more it *is* there. Not only is loneliness found to be far more common than previously believed, it is also increasingly linked with all sorts of nasty things: heart disease, dementia, strokes, and suicide. So serious has the problem become that governments are discovering it, to the extent that both Britain and Japan have Ministers of Loneliness, and Sweden has a Minister for Social Affairs. Many European countries, as well as the United States, are now devoting thought, time, and money to finding ways to combat loneliness, especially among the old, who suffer most from it.

Poets tried to describe sadness, loneliness, depression, long before those words entered the normal vocabulary of the educated person. Coleridge, one of the great English Romantic poets, was much given to sadness, his situation made worse by his addiction to opium, the drug of choice in the nineteenth century.

In his 'Dejection: an Ode', written more than two hundred years ago, he tried to explain what sadness and loneliness felt like. He spends the first lines of the poem describing the beauty of the night surrounding him, the crescent moon just rising, the air soft and serene. He studies it, acutely conscious of its beauty. And writes:

> I see them all, so excellently fair,
> I see, not feel, how beautiful they are!

And there it is, there it is. This is why we read poetry, to have a phrase, half a line of words, illuminate the world for us and sweep away all the blah blah blah and punch us in the heart with words we recognize instantly as the truth. We hear this voice, calling to us from two centuries ago, telling us what loneliness can do to our spirit, how it can damage our soul by limiting us to seeing when it is feeling that matters.

Addio

I must begin with a confession: my own exposure to the artistic expression of *'addio'* is primarily literary, for the need to say farewell to a loved person is one of the common tropes of literature, as it is of song and opera. In the normal course of events, people who love someone will leave the other person for periods of time, but most of these partings are based on the assumption that they will meet again, whether it's at the end of the day or after a longer separation. That's real life and day-to-day living, but day-to-day living is not what drama – certainly not what opera – is about. Verdi did not have *La Traviata*'s heroine, Violetta, stay at home and do the ironing, waiting for Alfredo to come home after a long day at the office, and Puccini certainly did not send Tosca and Cavaradossi out for a pizza and then have them settle onto the sofa for a night watching television. If their creators had presented them in this way, these vibrant characters would not have broken the hearts and exalted the spirits of opera-goers for so many years. Excess, we want excess.

In poetry, drama, and opera, the uncertainty that comes with saying farewell is filled with emotional turmoil: will we ever meet again? And if we do, will things be the same? This increases the dramatic tension and keeps the plot moving along. The uncertainty also creates the misunderstandings that lead to arias filled with suffering, jealousy, or rage. Or all three.

Those of you who are familiar with opera beyond the baroque era are familiar with many examples of departures that take place as a normal part of the drama and are often central to it, both dramatically and musically. In *Così fan tutte*, Mozart sends Guglielmo and Ferrando sailing off to war, while Fiordiligi and Dorabella swoon about, declaring their eternal love, and Don Alfonso seems to approve. The music is transportingly calm and tranquil, as if to underline the celestial harmony of women's fidelity: it is only later in the opera that the audience realizes that it was, instead, a hymn to the self-deceit of the lovers, perhaps of all lovers. In *La Bohème*, Puccini has Mimi and Rodolfo leave one another *'senza rancor'*. But are lovers capable, really, of leaving one another with no bad feelings?

Opera is not lodged in the mind only but also in the heart: we often go to the opera to watch the inventive staging of a drama and assess the quality of the dramaturgy, but we are there for the emotional charge as well. Much as the various elements of the performance might appeal to our minds, there is always the possibility – to some of us the hope – that they will assault our emotions too. Books, plays, poems give us a text that we hear or read in relative silence. Opera provides us the luxury of thought and reflection, but it also propels our emotions ever higher. The hero in a poem gives his battle cry and goes off to war. The same hero, transported to the world of opera, has his cry transformed into an aria that – using the magic of melody, harmony, rhythm, instrumentation, and the human voice – examines different emotions, creates various musical effects, and extends the dramatic and emotional turmoil for the entire length of the aria. And then he repeats the battle cry in the *da capo* part of the aria, after which he, his friends, his army, his beloved – and, if it's being performed at the Arena in Verona, all of the neighbours in a radius of half a kilometre – are caught up in the sound of trumpets and horns, and swept off – pulses pounding – to battle. I know it sounds ridiculous – the stories of opera often do – but one wonderful quality of opera is its ability to overcome its own inherent excess.

The addio scenes in opera, though often filled with heightened, excessive emotions, also serve to reveal character: this is what drama – and opera is, after all, drama – is meant to do. Addio scenes also present and reflect the ideals of the epoch in which the operas were written. The characters in baroque operas sing, in elegant language, of self-sacrifice, honour, nobility, and they almost always obey the superior demands of these obligations: Aeneas leaves Dido because his destiny calls him to go and found the new city, Rome, not because he has a new girlfriend. One has but to look at bel canto opera to see the way the change in popular values and ideals is reflected in the addio scene. In Donizetti's *Maria Stuarda*, the heroine calls her cousin, Elisabetta, Queen of England, a *'vil bastarda'* who brings shame on the throne of England. Instantly enraged, Elisabetta sends her off to her beheading: can there be a more final addio than this? Opera had moved into the Romantic era, taking the addio aria with it, but self-sacrifice, honour, and nobility had, to some degree, been left behind.

The examples I've given are from more modern operas, in the belief that they would be more easily recognized. The characters in baroque opera are no less ready to sing *addio* to the same things and often for the same reasons. They examine the pain and doubt that separation provokes; they give voice to the rage and despair that come from being abandoned and the equal agony of having to tell a lover to leave them. If nothing else, an addio aria leaves no doubt about who gets to say the last word.

In Memoriam

The last time I saw your mommy, we went walkies through a building in Washington being used as a gallery to show oil portraits of veterans from the various services in the war against Iraq who had been wounded in that effort.

The portraits were the work of former President George W. Bush. Presumably, he sat with his subjects for some time while painting them, listening to their stories, perhaps learning the manner in which they lost a limb, an eye, an organ, a physical capacity, their memory.

Shown were some of the 'Wounded Warriors', proud to have lost that or this for their country. I remember, I hope correctly, one portrait of a woman – I forget what branch she had served in – dancing with her remaining foot grounded on the floor while her dress swirled out to the tune, her new leg in the air, also taking part in the fun.

Your mother said nothing while we were inside: two old ladies walking slowly, arm in arm, through this show of selfless heroism.

As we passed outside, she paused for a moment and permitted herself to say: 'And the people responsible for this war feel no remorse, make no admission of guilt. Nothing.'

Ruth Bader Ginsburg
15 March 1933–18 September 2020